Mrs L. E. Stone

THROUGH
THE YEAR

with

Patience
Strong

LEOPARD

This edition first published in 1996 by Leopard,
a division of Random House UK Ltd,
20 Vauxhall Bridge Road,
London SW1V 2SA

Design by Mary Remnant

ISBN 0 7529 0328 4

January

Ring in the New

Let it come, the New Year that has come in through the door, whatever it may bring for us of good or bad in store.

Let it come and be welcome. We are ready to receive—the blessings and the challenges, because our hearts believe—that somewhere in the universe there is a God who cares—a God who walks beside us and a God who hears our prayers . . .

So greet the New Year with a song of joy and thankfulness—for the mercies of the past. Look up and onward press—day by day though hard the road. Keep going, never fear—Trust the One whose hand can lead you safely through the year.

The Gateways of the Year

What shall we take through the Gateways of the Year?
The staff of good hope and the lantern of good cheer . . .
A song in the heart—and on the lips a prayer—For dark
is the road and great the load we bear.

What shall we need for the journey we must take?
Endurance and faith and a courage none can break . . .
Keeping in view the vision bright and clear—Gladly we
pass through the Gateways of the Year.

JANUARY 3RD

Crumbs of Comfort

Only some scraps from the window thrown. A handful
of crumbs on the frosted stone—but they fed the birds
on a winter's day when the wind was cold and the sky
was grey. And so they survived to sing again—when
spring came dancing down the lane.

Only a few words kindly said—but someone was
strangely comforted—somebody desolate and
bereaved—was somehow blessed, consoled, relieved—
and once again to life was stirred—strengthened by a
timely word. Thus does God in mercy feed—His
children in their times of need.

The Ploughed Field

No golden corn waves in the wind; no crops grow, rich and green—And yet, there is a quiet beauty in this wintry scene: the furrowed acres newly ploughed; the fallow soil at rest. The slim black poplars silhouetted on the crimson west.

The field takes on a purple bloom that deepens into night—as the birds in dark flocks moving take their homeward flight . . . How lovely is this country scene. How restful to the eye: the bare brown earth beneath the glory of the evening sky.

JANUARY 5TH

Walking on a Winter's Day

The crunch of ice beneath your tread. The leafless branches overhead. A wayside cottage thatched with snow . . . The hedge with hips and haws aglow—becomes a strange and lovely sight—in the bright and frosty light.

Along the lanes you know so well—beauty casts a magic spell. There's so much to see and much to learn. At every gate and every turn—you see what summer's green concealed; the distant spire, the far-off field. For when the trees stand stripped and bare—they open windows everywhere . . . A different landscape you survey—walking on a winter's day.

The Sunrise of Another Year

In the depths of wintertime when all is bleak and grim and grey—January's bitter gloom is broken by a distant ray . . . We know that when December dies, though skies with snow be overcast—the shortest day has come and gone, the longest, darkest night has passed.

A far faint streak of golden light has fallen on the sleeping earth—and at this season, to the heart there comes the hint of hope's rebirth . . . This is the time of new beginnings, and though the day be cold and drear—This is a new and lovely morning. This is the sunrise of the year.

JANUARY 7TH

Sundial in the Snow

The sundial looks deserted standing deep in drifts of snow—It seems to say, what use am I when winds of winter blow? I cannot count the shining hours or tell the time for you, unless the sun be smiling, and the sky be fair and blue.

Standing in the wintry silence of its frozen dreams—thinking of the fire of summer, and the sun's warm beams . . . waiting for the new green life to quicken round its base, and the kiss of golden lips upon its stony face.

Bitter or Better

A bitter day or a better day. Which is it to be?
A shining day or a whining day. Gloom or gaiety . . .
A day for chewing grievances, poisoning the blood.
A day to look for something good or wallow in the
mud. A day for peace and quiet or for an argument.
A day to stir up trouble or to be content . . .
A day for turning discord into harmony. A bitter
day, a better day. Which is it to be?

JANUARY 9TH

The Promise

This is what the blackbird promised me—one bitter day
when all seemed cold and dead. He prophesied that one
day there would be—a canopy of blossom overhead—
and underfoot a carpet deep and bright—of primroses
and violets thickly spread. Where once snow lay
encrusted sugar-white—There'd be bluebells . . . This is
what he said.

I stood beside the frosted windowpane—and listened to
the thing he had to say. His golden notes came slipping
through the rain. The wind was rough, the sky was dark
and grey—and from his perch in branches bare and
black—He said—Though winter lingers grim and
long—One blue April morning I'll come back—and sing
to you a sweeter, lovelier song.

Piling Up

Feather-light the snowflakes fall and melt upon your face. Fairylike they flutter down like wisps of dainty lace . . . They seem to have no weight, no substance or solidity—yet sometimes on the widely spreading branches of a tree—they form a load too heavy for a straining bough to take—and underneath the crushing burden it will bend and break.

Like the snowflakes heaped upon the branches of the tree—troubles pile up on your mind until eventually— something breaks inside you underneath the leaden weight. So don't let worries weigh you down or cares accumulate. Deal with every problem as you meet it on the way. Carry only what you have the strength for, day by day.

Something to Show

Have something to show for the winter. Don't sit between supper and bed—contented with mere entertainment. Do something constructive instead. Create something useful or lovely—employing your hands and your brain—or study and set yourself lessons—new regions of knowledge to gain.

Those hours of the long winter evenings—much pleasure and profit can bring. Do something to prove you've not wasted—the months between Christmas and Spring.

JANUARY 12TH

Overburdened

Minute by minute throughout the night the snowflakes fall and weigh—gently and yet heavily on branch and twig and spray—and sometimes when the icy burden can't be shaken free—a laden bough will bend and break and spoil a lovely tree.

Minute by minute throughout our lives the world and its affairs—presses upon us with a weight of little fears and cares—that often prove too much for us unless we learn to pray—for wisdom sufficient to bear with joy the burdens of the day.

Happy Morning

Greet the day with happy heart and vow that it will be a well-lived and a worthwhile day. Accept it gratefully as a good and precious gift, a newly given chance to wrest a blessing out of every twist of circumstance.

Grey the day may look to you when first you wake to it. Don't go by appearance. Later on it may be lit with sunny gleams and golden dreams, adventure and romance. You must not judge a day by what it looks like at a glance.

Even though the day holds out no hope of happiness, don't despise it or despair for you can never guess what it may unfold before the sunset dies away. Greet with glad thanksgiving the beginning of each day.

The Heather Bank

On the frost-flecked rockery the winter heathers now are gay—bringing glory to the garden when the skies are drear and grey . . . When Summer clothes the moors with bloom, this bank is bare and colourless—But now, before the snowdrop comes, it has its hour of loveliness. In between the weathered stones the vivid clumps of heather grow—lilac-tinted, mauve and purple, rosy pink and white as snow . . . And looking at this flowery bank when cold winds flow and grey fog chills—I walk again in memory the tracks that thread the heathered hills.

JANUARY 15TH

Winter Wheat

Like a green mist on the field the winter wheat appears, and in the far faint song of harvest echoes in our ears; just a down of tender shoots upon the frosted soil—fair reward for early sowing, trouble, time and toil. When winds are bleak and bitter and the pale sun gives no heat; it cheers the spirit when we see a field of wheat.

The Gardener's Friend

Here he comes, the perky robin with his gay red
breast—He perches on the barrow, absolutely self-
possessed . . . Looking for a snack perhaps, his
dinner or his tea. But I'm inclined to think he likes
a bit of company.

He carries on a conversation, chirping, twittering—
making friendly observations—idly gossiping . . .
And whether it is warm and fine or winter cold and
grey—He comes around to have a chat and pass
the time of day.

Before the Thrushes Sing

Outside it is wintertime, a world all grey and cold, but
inside there is colour: rose and crimson, blue and gold.
Bulbs in bowls on every sill have burst out into bloom—
and brought a warm rich glow into the January gloom.

Daffodils with brazen trumpets lift their regal heads.
Hyacinths in gorgeous tones of pinks and mauves and
reds. Crocus candles burning brightly, tulips stiff and
proud. Snowdrops pale as ghosts amongst the bold and
brilliant crowd.

Let the wind blow wild and keen against the frosted
pane. Let the weather do its worst! Come blizzard,
snow or rain—April to my window comes before
the thrushes sing. Outside it is wintertime, but inside
it is spring.

JANUARY 18TH

Shine, Sun, Shine

Glitter through the trees that lean above the ice-locked
streams. Through the aisles of copse and forest shed
your magic beams . . . Steal into the cracks and wrinkles
of the earth's old face. Light up every nook and corner
of this wintry place. Shimmer on the frosted pools along
the frozen lane. Shine, Sun, shine upon the world! And
make it smile again.

The Orchard

How strange it is in Wintertime! The trees stand stark
and still—Bough-deep in the curling mists that roll up,
grey and chill—from the sodden water-meadows. Can
this be the place—where on April mornings rosy
branches interlace—Where blackbirds tune their silver
flutes to notes of ecstasy—and thrushes in the twilight
sing their sweetest melody . . . Through this place of
seeming death a wind of life will blow. Through these
black and sapless boughs a tide of green will flow.
Haloed in a cloud of blossom every tree will stand—
Quickened into sudden beauty by some unseen hand.

Let Life Begin Anew

Every day that's granted you let life begin again. Do not cling to memories that leave a stab of pain. Never hold on to a grudge that rankles in the heart. Every day a new adventure and another start.

Never ruin in advance your chances of success—by brooding thoughts of failure and unhappiness. Don't invite more trouble if you want to get along—by constantly remembering the things that went all wrong.

Make amends for past mistakes while there is time to try. Do not leave it till tomorrow lest the chance slip by . . . Let the dawn ring up the curtain on a lovely view. Every day get up and say that life begins anew.

A Winter Walk

Down the winding lane we go, beneath the elms where black rooks crowd. Gold light filters through the branches as the pale sun breaks a cloud . . . Past the lychgate of the church—across the bridge beside the mill—Lingering a moment here to see the stream slip down the hill.

Past the cottage on the corner in its garden, snug and neat. Through the gate into the field, now striped with green of winter wheat . . . Pausing, poised against the wind, to watch the hills go grey with rain. On along the wood's dark edge . . . then up the road, and home again.

The Time Has Come

The longest night has passed away, the shortest day has come and gone. The sun's low arc is widening. The light will linger from now on . . . Slowly imperceptibly, at first you will not notice it—but the days of January lengthen slightly bit by bit—until there comes an afternoon when suddenly you are aware—of a radiance at the window and a brightness in the air—for a space of minutes only, then the glory fades away. It is like a vision granted with the ending of the day.

The wintry world around you lies, the frozen puddles shine like glass—but you know the time has come to look for snowdrops in the grass.

Yesterdays and Tomorrows

God of my yesterdays, I have forgotten
All that I failed in when put to the test.
Yet somewhere the whole of my life is recorded
Things unremembered and still unconfessed.
Time buries much and the years fly so fast,
I'll need Thy forgiveness if judged on the past.

God of the future and times not yet planned
All my tomorrows still rest in Thy hand;
The moments, the hours and the days yet to be
Are veiled from my view but are known unto Thee . . .
Thou seest the place where the road will be hard.
Go Thou before me, my Guide and my Guard.

The Very Place

Was this the wood where the bluebells grew in the lovely month of May? Was this the lane where the primroses clustered all along the way? Was this the garden where roses blazed—pink, lemon, cream and red? Was this the meadow where sheets of yellow buttercups were spread?

Was this the orchard where thrushes sang amongst the apple trees? Was this the field where the ripe corn rustled in the summer breeze? Was this the pond where the lilies floated in the golden light—and where I watched the fairy wings of dragonflies in flight?

The very place, yes the very place. But how different today! The scene has changed to a dreary world. All the colour has drained away. It is hard to imagine as here I stand and watch the winter gale, that this is the window where once I stood to hear the nightingale.

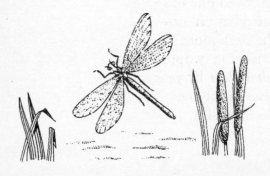

The Silent Garden

Silent now the garden lies
Under dark and stormy skies.
Days are short and nights are long,
Frosts are sharp and winds are strong . . .
One by one the petals fall
From the last rose on the wall.
Winter's breath is in the air;
Birds are mute and boughs are bare.

Yet no bitter tear we shed,
For we know they are not dead.
We, with faith unquestioning,
Say there'll be another Spring.
At the end of Winter's reign,
In the garden once again,
There'll be blossom on the spray.
None can take this hope away.

Why then should our faith sink low,
When some loved one has to go
Out into the great unknown—
Out into the dark alone?
Death the victor may appear.
But remember, year by year,
New sap rises in the tree.
Life goes on eternally.

Looking at the Garden

Looking through the window at a garden bleak and bare—it's wonderful to think of all the treasure buried there: the dormant life in root and bulb. It is the strangest thing—that, like a vault, the soil holds fast the riches of the spring . . . In a secret hiding place the wealth is stored away—until the moment comes when it is bought out for display.

The day when from an earthy grave, now damp and dark and cold—the sun will bring out crocuses of ivory and gold . . . It seems well nigh impossible that there should ever be—daffodils along the path and blossom on the tree.

In Someone's Prayers

It's only in the winter we appreciate the glow—of blazing coals and burning logs. It's only then we know—the comfort and the blessing of a warm and cosy room. Beside the firelit hearth we can forget the outside gloom.

And so it is in life, it's not till troubles come along—your realize what friendship means. It's not till things go wrong—you know how good it is to feel that you're in someone's prayers—in time of sorrow and distress to know somebody cares . . . You take it all for granted when a sunlit way you wend—but when it's winter in the heart you thank God for a friend.

If the Heart Is Singing

If the heart is singing you cannot go far wrong—
for you will discover there's magic in a song
that scares away the demons that throng around us all,
wanting us to stumble and to see us fall.

If the heart is singing nothing can get through—
only that which strengthens and what is best for you.

Let the world go grumbling and grinding on its way,
 for you'll have the secret that lights the common day.
You'll see the hidden glory behind the leaden cloud.
 Lightly you will travel, head high and back unbowed,
 for when the heart is singing the soul is singing too.
Your sins will be forgiven, for every day is new.

Solo

Alone upon the leafless bough a blackbird sang a song. The sky was grey and wintry but his note was sweet and strong. No company, encouragement or coaxing did he need—no cue, no audience to applaud, no prompting and no lead.

Alone he sang for pure delight and as I listened there— There came the thought that Love too sings where all is bleak and bare—its nature to express in face of malice and mistrust. Love unprompted, gives itself and sings because it must . . . meeting the unspoken need with charity and grace—like the bird that sings impromptu in a lonely place.

Somebody's Tomorrow

Is anyone the happier for meeting you today? Has anyone been prayed for just because he came your way?

Has anyone been helped because you stopped to lend a hand—spared a little time to listen, tried to understand?

Has anyone been made to feel that God was somewhere near? Has someone somewhere been relieved of worry and of fear?. . . Has someone rediscovered faith in what is good and true—seen another side to life, another point of view?

If the answer's Yes, then you have earned your night's repose. If No, your day was wasted, spent in vain— and at its close—there can be no satisfaction; not unless you say—that somebody's tomorrow will be better than today.

A Blessing and a Promise

Softly, imperceptibly the snowflakes fall and spread—
a warm and lovely blanket on the living and the
dead. The kindly years like snowflakes fall and
cover quietly—the bitterness that lies within the
grave of memory.

Winter does not last for ever nor does grief remain—
when Time has done its healing work and Spring has
come again . . . Love lives on and Life comes back the
spirit to renew—wherever there's an open door to let
the glory through.

Nigh two thousand years ago the Saviour came to
bring—a promise and a blessing to the sad and
sorrowing . . . He alone can calm the heart and lift the
sunken head. "Blessed are they who mourn", said He,
"for they shall be comforted."

February

FEBRUARY 1ST

Quiet Is My Garden

Quiet is my garden now. No sign of life appears. Quiet as my heart beneath the snowflakes of the years.

Time will melt the frosts of grief. The wintry days will pass. The thaw will come and shoots of hope be scattered in the grass—And I shall discover God has planted there for me—for my comfort and my joy: the flowers of Memory.

FEBRUARY 2ND

The Acrobats

I love to watch the bluetit with his primrose-tinted front—turning crazy somersaults. It's like a circus stunt . . . Upside down he hangs and pecks a juicy bit of fat. No mistake about it, he's a first class acrobat.

Watch him with the monkey nuts. He has the greatest fun. He swings and clings and picks the precious nuts out one by one. Agile as a star performer on a high trapeze—he jerks and wiggles, twists and wriggles with the utmost ease—and when a bit of coconut is hung out on the tree—with his claws he gets a grip and nibbles skilfully. It's as if he sets out to amuse and entertain. I do believe he knows we're watching at the windowpane.

The Whisperers

I thought that snow had fallen overnight—when I saw
the willow ringed with white—like a necklace looped
around the tree. Mystified, I crossed the lawn to see—
snowdrops. Yes, the snowdrops back again—bright with
beaded drops of frozen rain.

Every year it happens. Every year—And yet when first
I look and see them here—they always seem to take
me by surprise—when winter's pall hangs heavy
from the skies . . . Too soon, I say. But as I stoop to
stare at the little flowerlets swinging there—I catch the
whispered message that they bring—and hail them as
the harbingers of Spring.

Sunset

That belt of trees when clothed in leafy green—rose like
a wall, a solid massive screen—that hid from my sight
the hills beyond the town, so I never saw the summer
sun go down.

But now with every branch and bough stripped bare—I
can see the glory over there: the rose, the gold, the purple and the red—the fire across the far horizon spread.

Compensation for the winter days! To sit at dusk
and watch the sunset blaze—crumbling to ash until
the last red spark—is quenched with the sudden onset
of the dark.

I Am the Way

Footprints make tracks in the untrodden snow. Pathways for others. We none of us know—where we shall be at the end of the day—so follow the One who said, I am the Way.

Follow the marks that He left on the road—for all who were staggering under a load. Follow the feet that were nailed to a cross—through trouble, temptation and failure and loss.

He on the untrodden snow of the years—has marked out for us with the blood and the tears—the path of salvation, for did He not say—I am the Life and the Truth and the Way?

Artificial Flowers

Lovely are the artificial flowers they make today. Fresh and natural they look in colours bright and gay. Petals, stalks and leaves deceive the eye. You have to feel—to find out if they are a fake or if they're truly real.

Some dislike them, but in winter are they not a boon, bringing into cold grey days a memory of June? You don't object to flowers in pictures or on tapestry—so why despise these works of art? Quite perfect they can be.

But when upon the earth the living flowers of spring are spread—you realize the difference. The man-made ones look dead. And is it not a paradox that starts you wondering why—the flowers you love the best of all are those that have to die?

Cheerfulness

Cheerfulness is like a lamp that radiates a light—scattering depressing thoughts and putting fears to flight—generating happiness whenever felt or heard—with an optimistic viewpoint or a cheery word.

Cheerfulness can animate the spirit of a crowd. Something happens as when sun comes breaking through a cloud . . . Some there are who have this power to be a medium—that the joy of life flows through whenever troubles come—changing situations when the atmosphere is tense—knowing how to strike the note of hope and confidence.

FEBRUARY 8TH

Muted Violin

When the east wind cuts like a sharp edged knife—and the black frost bites in the raw grey dawn—The trees feel no tremor of quickened life—No green thing out of the earth is drawn.

The iron claw of Winter grips root and spray. The thrush is reluctant his song to begin—And the music of Spring seems as far away—as the note of a muted violin.

Watching the Sun Go Down

Sometimes after fog and frost and skies of leaden grey—
there comes a lovely sunset like a blessing on the day.
Through the leafless trees you see the red and rosy
rays—and before you draw the curtains on the dying
blaze—you pause a moment, thinking of the wonder of
it all: the great world turning from the brightness of
that burning ball—away from all the warmth, the
power, the glory and the light—wheeling back into the
darkness that we call the night.

Nothing Wasted, Nothing Lost

Bare is the oak this winter's day and black the boughs against the sky. Round the stripped and sapless branches, no leaf dances, no birds fly—And yet I know it is not dead. It waits, conforming patiently—to the laws that operate in Nature's wise economy.

Nothing is wasted, nothing lost. Bark and twigs and withered leaves—rot around the spreading roots and thus the hungry soil receives—the food it needs to feed and nourish next year's growth. How wonderful! In this silent process lies a lesson and a parable.

As in nature, so with us. We too, can learn to recreate—life from death and joy from sorrow, strength from weakness, love from hate . . . We, like the trees, must suffer change when Time brings storm and bitter frost—but we out of evil can bring goodness . . . Nothing is wasted, nothing lost.

Look For the Best

Look for the best and not the worst in everyone you meet – the friend who knocks upon your door, the stranger in the street . . . Look for the beauty not the flaws in every character—the good intention not the bad, the kindness, not the slur.

Close an eye to faults and failings. You have failings too. Pray that God will do the same and not be hard on you—noting your redeeming points, and not remembering every little weakness in the day of reckoning.

That's our only hope of coming through the final test— the hope that we'll be judged not by the worst but the best . . . If the Lord ignored our virtues, seeing just the vice—Who would ever get beyond the gates of Paradise?

Winter's Gift

Bone bare trees against a sullen sky. Fog and frost and wet winds shrieking by. Raw dark mornings and tracks of rutted mire—leading to hayrick, stable, barn and byre.

This is the winter in the country's heart—a grey isolation in a world apart—but this, too, is winter as the long night falls: the flicker of firelight on familiar walls.

There is a healing in the winter's mood. Sated on summer's ripened plenitude—I walk in the quiet fields—and gratefully feed on the gleanings of austerity.

Underneath the Earth

Underneath the earth the bulbs lie deep,
Buried in their winter sleep.
Under the frosts the seeds are sealed
In garden bed and furrowed field.
Under a shroud of seeming death
They wait for April's warming breath:
Iris, tulips, crocuses,
Daffodils, anemones.

In the hard unyielding ground,
The sapless roots are locked and bound.
Below the crust of morning time,
Nature dormant bides her time.
Lilac, lily, cherry, may
Await their resurrection day.

Early Song

A Throstle from the topmost branches of a cherry tree—
floods the leafless orchard with a stream of melody . . .
Who, I wonder, taught this bird his sweet and liquid
note? Strange that music such as this could come from
one small throat.

What deep impulse moves him to that song of joy
divine? He must have guessed it is the month of good
Saint Valentine—And so he tries a scale or two to exercise his voice—Practising a love-song for the lady of his
choice.

Strength of Will

What became of all the vows you made the other day?
You meant them at the time but your intentions died
away. The New Year lost its sparkle and the thrill
went out of it. Old habits got a grip again. You gave
in bit by bit.

You hadn't got the strength of will to carry you along.
The will needs constant exercise to keep it firm and
strong—so every day do something to employ the idle
will—make it work by giving it some purpose to fulfil.
All our failings can be kept within the will's control. It
is the spine of character: the backbone of the soul.

While You're Waiting

While you're waiting for tomorrow, get the best out of
today.
While you're waiting for the sunshine don't complain at
skies of grey.
While you wait for future pleasures don't forget the
ones you've had.
Call to mind the things enjoyed, the happy times and
not the sad.

While you're waiting for the granting of the wish you
hold most dear,
Don't lose sight of all the joys that life can offer now
and here.
Times of waiting can be fruitful and to you much good
can bring.
Make the winter yield a blessing while you're waiting
for the Spring.

FEBRUARY 17TH

Trees in the Wind

The oak tree, proud and ancient, and the sapling thin
and frail—sway beneath the driving winds and bow
before the gale . . . Bending, but not breaking, as the
storm goes raving past—Resisting not the force and
fury of the bitter blast.

The winds of God blow round the world and sorrows
come to all—But if we bow to Providence we shall not
fail or fall—Knowing that there is some final purpose
to fulfil—Finding strength in yielding to His good and
perfect will.

FEBRUARY 18TH

In Time

No life stirs in the frozen clods—No shoot of green
breaks through the mould. No wing of bird beats in
the hush and all the world is grey and cold.

The distant hills are domed with snow; the hedges white
with morning rime—But buds will break and life awake,
and Spring return, in God's good time.

Daphne

The dainty little daphne bush that stands beside the gate—Opens out her rosy buds before the blackbirds mate . . . Putting on her gay pink blossoms as the winter wanes—challenging the bitter frosts, the wild winds and the rains.

Flinging wide her fragrant perfume as the breeze goes by—she comforts every weary heart and gladdens every eye . . . Telling us that soon the flowers will bloom and song-birds sing—Loveliest of all the lovely messengers of spring.

Just a Little

A little help goes a long long way when it's just the help you need. A little word quite a lot can say—one little word can feed—your hungry heart with a single crumb when you sit alone with your tears—wondering what became of all the lost and lonely years.

One little morsel of broken bread an aching void can fill—and send you out with your strength renewed to climb the next great hill . . . One little measure of kindliness can calm and comfort you—and bring you out of the pit to find the world made fresh and new.

Laugh at Yourself

Laugh at yourself when you're breaking your heart over something quite small. Laugh at yourself when you're making a fuss over nothing at all—failing to see what is funny—and taking the pessimist's view—laugh at yourself in the mirror and see what a smile does for you. Laugh at yourself when you're trying to reach for the moon in the sky—and laugh when you find yourself sighing for something too big and too high . . . Laugh at yourself for assuming that life would go always your way. You never can tell—but all will be well if you laugh at yourself every day.

FEBRUARY 22ND

February Eves

Between the daylight and the dark on February eves— The dusk comes in a smoky haze; a blue light falls—and weaves a web of magic round the town. There is a sense of change. The houses in the little streets look beautiful and strange . . . Only for a moment, then the vision dies away—fading with the fading light of the departing day.

The Evergreens

How bare would be my garden now—how desolate and drear the scene—if through the rain I could not see the beauty of the evergreen.

The pine and cedar, fir and yew stretch forth their boughs in Winter-time—as if to hide the nakedness of ash and maple, birch and lime.

When God made trees He must have known how we should miss the leafy sprays—and so He made the evergreens to cheer us through the sunless days.

Take Your Time

Take your time—or time takes you and drains your strength away. Take a minute, maybe two, throughout your busy day—for slowing down to meditate—from worldly things apart—in a quiet place to wait with a receptive heart. Take your time to think about the greatest things of all—take your time to work it out before the curtains fall.

Why the worry? What's the hurry? Take your time and stroll—picking from life's wayside hedges that which feeds the soul . . . Take your time and walk on grass; to look at flowers and trees—wandering and pondering on wonders such as these . . . Slacken pace to see the view. Take your time or time takes you.

The Sun

After many bitter weeks of ice and frost and snow—the sun is like the smile of God upon the world below. You lift your face to feel the glow and as it shines on you—the glory and the power of it you realise anew.

Suddenly there come these moments when you are aware—of how wonderful it is, that ball of fire up there—that draws the green shoot from the dark where winter's course has run—and with a joy akin to worship you salute the sun.

Come Back

Come back, swallow, to the nest you loved—Beneath the cottage eaves—I miss the flutter of your beating wings—about the ivy leaves.

Come back soon upon the winds of Spring—some good and lovely day—when there is blossom in the lilac hedge and red buds on the may.

Under the Shadow of a Guiding Hand

We do not always see the way ahead. We do not always know which path to tread. This is the point at which we need to light the lamp of Faith to take into the night.

Trust and believe that God is leading you to a fulfilment hidden from your view. Know only good can come of what is planned, under the shadow of that guiding hand.

It is not always granted us to see—what lies behind the present mystery. Waste not words in asking why or where. Time will unfold the answer to your prayer.

Beautiful Moments

I opened wide the window to the morning of the day—
and from the wintry branches of the trees across the
way—I heard the robins and the thrushes fluting
joyously—and it seemed that they were singing specially
for me.

I stood and listened. Every note was like a silver bell—
and deep inside my heart I knew: I knew that all was
well. A word of hope had reached me through the birds
. . . I can't explain—But that lovely message has not
come to me in vain. A thrill of new expectant life along
my nerves had run—as, looking up, I felt the warm
sweet kisses of the sun.

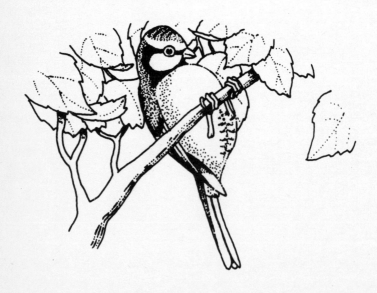

March

The Bend by the Signpost

We've turned the bend by the signpost that bears the word to Spring—We've come a few steps nearer to the moment that will bring—the hallelujah choruses to garden, wood and lane—telling us that life is stirring in the soil again.

We've turned our backs on Winter though still the winds blow cold—we see beneath the budding tree a flash of fairy gold. Daffodils and crocuses are massing out of sight—preparing for the festival of colour, life and light. This is the month of miracles, the season of rebirth—when beauty breaks the seals and springs triumphant from the earth.

The Garden

Now for the garden, the weeding, the growing. The raking, the staking, the planting, the sowing . . . Now for the jobs that are waiting for you. You wonder just how you will ever get through.

Now for the garden you saw in your dreams—when you were weaving those wonderful schemes. You grumble a bit when it takes all your leisure—but you admit there is no greater pleasure—than starting again when the Spring comes around—working out there on your own bit of ground.

Here They Are!

I remember an autumn day, when the wind was keen and the sky was grey—I planted crocuses at the edge of the border that runs by the hawthorn hedge.

Then came the winter with snow piled high—So bitter the weather I feared they'd die, but the snow served to keep them safe and warm—sheltered from dangers of frost and storm . . . And now here they are with their buds unrolled—edging the lawn with a braid of gold!

Always a Surprise

We know it's going to happen but it's always a surprise—when green tips poke out of the earth and point towards the skies . . . First the dainty snowdrop, then the crocus white and gold—then the early daffodils preparing to unfold.

At the gates of Lent they stand, the heralds of the Spring—before the blackbird and the thrushes really start to sing . . . While winter fires still crackle and its fogs hang in the air—they seem to come up overnight and take us unaware.

We never grow accustomed to this annual miracle. Year by year we see it but it's always wonderful. We never quite believe it till it's there before our eyes. Every year it happens but it's always a surprise.

Crocus

The first to come! . . . The golden crocus, boldly thrusting up—as if to catch and hold the sunlight in its painted cup—The first ones out to shout a salutation of good cheer—making haste to show themselves before the rest appear.

For soon will come the other members of the family—robed in deepest purple, palest mauve and ivory—and dazzled by their beauty we'll forget to say goodbye—to the first that took the risk, and braved the wintry sky.

MARCH 6TH

Reluctance

Reluctantly Spring makes her way—At Winter's edge she hesitates, as if she feared to come too soon. The primrose halts, the windflower waits—for Spring's green cloak is flecked with snow, and in her tresses wild and bright—a dew of frost glints in the gold and sparkles in the sun's cold light.

Be Your Own Best Friend

Be your own best friend. A friend—and not an enemy—
so that if you're left alone you're in good company—
Learn to love the silences that steal in here and there—
as you sit and think your thoughts before an empty chair.

Know yourself and teach yourself contentedly to live—
independent of the world and what it has to give . . .
Train your mind to gather gold from every passing
day—so that you will never have to wish the hours away.

Come to terms and to yourself a good companion be—
one to be relied upon when life is out of key . . .
Loneliness you'll never know and peace you will possess—if you have within yourself the root of happiness.

A New Note

There's a new note in the choirs that sing upon the leafless boughs. There's a new song in the air to-day—
a song that seems to rouse—and resurrect the life
within, grown cold in winter hours—Waking all the
old sweet dreams—of blossom, buds and flowers.

There's a new hope in the world to-day because of
this glad sound. There's an urgent and an upward
thrust of green things in the ground. There's a new joy
in the hearts of men because of this strange note: this
rapturous reveille from some little feathered throat.

MARCH 9TH

Bubbles in the Sky

How lovely are the clouds of March—under heaven's
spreading arch! Foamy chariots riding by—across the
highways of the sky . . . Upward we look surprised to
see—so huge a mass move suddenly—like a thousand
flags unfurled—above the mountains of the world.

And when a driving wind prevails—they resemble
billowing sails—dipping across the waves of space—as
if competing in a race . . . Feather-light the big clouds
break—Bursting like bubbles they froth and flake—floating off into the blue—beyond the measure of our view.

There All the Time

They were there all the time in the frozen clay. They were down in the dark where the thick frost lay, but I could not believe they would come again—as I sought for them there in the wintry lane.

And now they are here where my snow-boots trod: primroses fresh from the hand of God . . . A carpet of yellow and green I see—mocking my incredulity.

Just like the blessings we long to find—when we are troubled in heart and mind—blessings like primroses hidden from view—They were there all the time . . . but we never knew.

Something in the Heart

There is something in the heart that keeps us strong and sane—in the hour of peril, of temptation and of pain— Bids us cling to life in spite of sorrow and of loss— pointing to the light behind the shadow of the cross.

There is something in the soul that yearns to spread its wings—with the wild desire to breathe the breath of higher things—something that abhors all evil, ugliness and strife—and responds to truth and goodness, beauty, love and life.

Underneath the outward show of personality—lies the holy part of us that lives eternally—This spiritual consciousness that no man can define—that changes human nature with a touch of the divine.

Best Points

Look out for the best points in others,
Look out for the finest things first . . .
Be sure that you've found all the good traits
Before recognising the worst.

Too often, put out by some quarrel
Past kindness we're apt to forget
The ties of affection are severed
By words that we live to regret.

And many a friendship is broken,
Because when it comes to the test
We see only what are the worst points
And fail to remember the best.

Would You Believe It?

Would you believe it? It's happened again—the gold hazel catkins are out in the lane. The crocuses making bright lakes in the grass—ripple like waves as the stormy winds pass.

The chiffchaff is building. The aconites glow—like stars in the woods where the swelling brooks flow. The winter is passing. I sense on the breeze—the stirring of life in the roots of the trees . . . The daffodils eager to dance into view—are poised and are ready, awaiting their cue. The spirit of Springtime has tapped on the pane. Would you believe it? It's happened again.

Twice as Wonderful

The blackbird sings a sweeter song when winter has
been hard and long. The daffodils all gay and bold,
lifting trumpets bright as gold—seem to make a lovelier
show when they have slept beneath the snow.

The primrose opening again on the banks along the
lane—looks more beautiful to me—and violets smell
more heavenly—if the weather has been bleak . . . If
day by day and week by week—I've looked through
frosted panes and seen—no gleam of sun, no touch of
green. When winter has been terrible – the spring seems
twice as wonderful!

MARCH 15TH

Tiny Travellers

Hosts of tiny travellers will soon be on their way—
winging to the shores of Britain for their summer stay . . .
From their haunts in lands afar unnumbered miles
they'll fly—following the secret tracks across the
boundless sky.

Here is something strange and baffling to the human
brain. We know the chiffchaff will appear, and swallows
come again—But how and why we cannot say. No big
and clever words—can explain the mystery of the
migrating birds.

Blow, March Wind!

Blow, March wind, as hard as you will. Your teeth are sharp and your breath is chill. Your voice is strident and harsh and shrill . . . but I've seen the green point of a daffodil.

So what do I care for your buffeting? Did I not hear a chiffchaff sing? At the stormy heart of your blustering— is heard the first faint note of spring.

Blow, March wind, cold and bitter and wet. Rough and unfriendly you are and yet—I laugh in your face and defy your threats—knowing you bring me violets.

MARCH 17TH

Lost

Lost between daybreak and sundown—the hour that I idled away. Gold from Time's treasury squandered. One precious hour of the day.

Sixty good minutes I wasted. Where did they go ? Where indeed? Minutes I'll never recover—minutes that someday I'll need.

Life does not tick on forever—as all have to learn to their cost . . . We cannot recapture a moment—or call back the time that we lost.

At Last

At last there is a flush of green upon the wayside hedge. At last I've seen a primrose out along the meadow's edge . . . At last beside the garden path the crocus candles blaze—purple, gold and ivory, to light the Lenten days.

At last there is a rosy haze upon the almond trees—and the first gay daffodils are dancing in the breeze . . . At last the birds are nesting . . . There's a new note in the air—the hidden pulse of quickened life is beating everywhere.

Still the gales blow cold and keen against the cottage pane—but something that I thought was dead has stirred in me again . . . A strange excitement warms the blood, my heart begins to sing—for as the March wind rushes by me—I can smell the spring.

MARCH 19TH

The Storm Cock

What does he care for the shrieking gale—the blustering
gusts and the driving hail . . . High in the tossed and
straining tree—He sings his song defiantly.

Scorning the hedgerows safe and warm—seeking no
shelter from the storm—Tuning his note to the wind's
high scream—bent on pursuing his own set theme.

MARCH 20TH

The Hidden Corners

Dust gets into hidden corners where it can't be seen—
and when in spring you give your home that necessary
clean—that is where you'll find it when you start to
search about. The places that are not included when
you're turning out. The jobs you have no time for when
you're on the daily round. The spots not under notice.
That is where the dust is found!

Minds, like rooms, have hidden places where no sunbeams play—where dust blows in and cobwebs form
and grow from day to day. So don't neglect these secret
corners; let the light get in. Open wide the inner windows on the world within. Clear out all the grievances,
sweep ugly fears away, then start afresh and try to have
a spring-clean every day.

Open the Window

Open the window and let in the sun.
The season of life and of light has begun.
Open the window. The wind is a broom
that sweeps out the cobwebs, the dust and the gloom.

Open the windows of hope. Fling them wide,
when it is cheerless and stuffy inside . . .
Germs of self-pity, of fear and of doubt
thrive in the darkness, so drive them all out.

Viewed from the shadows through windows shut fast,
the future is veiled in the fogs of the past . . .
But eyes that can see with a faith big and bold
look through the mists to horizons of gold.

Power of Happiness

When the mind is happy the heart is happy too. Picking up the message, the body takes its cue—and the feet, responding, walk with lighter tread—as thoughts like merry dancers go whirling round your head.

Brightness, like sunshine, sparkles in your eyes. Somehow you feel better as your spirits rise . . . Hope and health together blend in harmony—Nervous tensions slacken, calmly, quietly.

Cheerfulness works wonders. Gaiety can be—potent as a tonic. Nature's remedy—for the ills and ailments that weaken and depress. Simple but effective; the power of happiness.

Flowers in the Window

In a dark and squalid alley under leaden skies—
The sight of flowers upon the sill would come as a
surprise—even if the blackened walls had not been
blitzed and scarred—for Beauty cannot tarry long where
life is grim and hard.

Yet, there it was! . . . A splash of gold upon the grimy
glass—Like a challenge boldly flung to all who chanced
to pass . . . conjuring the strangest scene beneath the
smoky sky: daffodils . . . a lakeside path—and
Wordsworth walking by!

Someone in that ugly house had caught the sun's pale
gleam. Someone in that gloomy rom had dared to
dream a dream . . . Someone, wiser than they knew,
had done a lovely thing—and brought into that ruined
street the magic of the Spring.

Just in Time

Just in time is time enough for setting matters straight—
because if you are just in time you cannot be too late—
for patching up a quarrel when bad feelings have been
stirred—burying the hatchet with a letter or a word.

Tomorrow is a day too late to mend a broken heart,
or to save a friendship when the bonds have come
apart . . . Today the severed links you can repair and
reunite. Today you may be just in time to put the
wrong things right.

Daffodils in the Market

On the market stall they lay: a blaze of gold against the
grey: how they came, and where they grew—no one
bothered; no one knew.

But their beauty caught the eye, and startled every
passer-by . . . Folk went their way, hearts light, hopes
high—and never guessed the reason why.

Looking Forward

Be a looker-forward and not a looker-back. Be a presser-onward upon life's stony track. Don't waste time regretting the things you cannot mend. Anticipate good fortune at every twist and bend.

Keep going, never doubting the outcome of your dreams. Have faith in their fulfilment. Though dark the future seems—Believe that somewhere somehow God's purpose will unfold—and the grey horizon be turned to blue and gold.

Give thanks for every blessing, your job, your home, your friends. Don't take these things for granted. A grateful spirit lends—a glory and a meaning to pathways drear and dun. Expect a bright tomorrow and turn towards the sun.

Perfect

Perfect are the lovely daffodils—arrayed in bowls
along my windowsills—with graceful stalks and
trumpets glowing gold—yet such perfection somehow
leaves me cold.

I cannot help but look beyond the pane—to watch
the wild ones swaying in the rain . . . Like ballerinas
whirling in the breeze—to blackbird-music from the
apple trees.

My indoor beauties proud and stately stand. The
catalogue was right . . . They're really grand—and yet
my heart they will never entrance—because I like a
daffodil to dance!

Almond Blossom

Almond blossom once again! Fairy scenes in street and lane. In the bleak and bitter days, on the stark and leafless sprays—rosy buds uncurl and bring—promise of another Spring.

By the wall the old trees lean—where through winter there has been—a dark and tangled tracery . . . And now, this loveliness I see: a cloud of palest tint and tone—upon the grey time-mellowed stone; a cloud of bloom, so beautiful—it might be called a miracle.

Wonderful Blessings

With praise and thanksgiving I greet this good day—for wonderful blessings are coming my way . . .The things I have prayed for and worked for I see—on the horizon now coming to me.

For what is imagined in heart and in mind—you form in reality and you will find—they'll take shape in time. So be patient; believe. That harvest you'll reap and those blessings receive.

How Did it Happen?

Violets by the woodland way. Promise of blossom on
the spray. Wonderful glow of daffodils—underneath the
windowsills—and by the verges of the lane—primroses
beaded with the rain.

Glorious splash of crocus gold—as in the sun the cups
unfold. Thrusting of tips where frosts still cling. Wonder
of hyacinths opening. Fragrance of daphne on the
breeze. Beautiful pink of almond trees. Just as if somebody overnight—had cast a spell and lit a light—by
some act of wizardry. How did it happen? You tell me.

MARCH 31ST

Nature Laughs

Bitter is the wind of March and cold its Lenten
breath—but it sounds the knell that tells the world
of Winter's death—if you listen quietly you'll hear a
blackbird sing—telling you that God once more has
sent another Spring.

At its gate the blossom burst in clouds of white
and rose—and along the garden path the daffodils
unclose . . . Nature laughs, but Man in glum and
discontented mood—has no time for song of praise or
word of gratitude.

Lent

As the Winter nears its end there come the Lenten
days. Watching at the inner gate with fasting, prayer
and praise—we search into our inmost faith new
meanings to distil. Denying self and strengthening
the fibres of the will.

Wise and shrewd is Mother Church. She knows how
much we need—to curb the enemies within: self–pity,
pride, sloth, greed . . . The will grows slack and flabby
if it's never exercised. The seven deadly sins, although
in modern dress disguised are with us still, so it is good
to set this time apart—for the feeding of the soul, the
cleansing of the heart.

Luxuries

Do not say there's nothing you can give up during
Lent. Give up being angry when there's something
you resent. Give up giving in to the temptation to hit
out—to lose your temper when provoked and throw
your weight about.

Deny yourself the luxury of nursing grievances.
The pleasure of complaining over petty nuisances.
The satisfaction of revenge when hurt in any way—
blaming others, striking back or making someone pay.

Give up giving way to moods when clouds hang over
you, feeling sorry for yourself, depressing others too . . .
These are luxuries indeed on which so much is spent.
Try to do without them as an exercise for Lent.

Fasting

Most of us are overfed, so fasting in these days—does
not mean so very much, but there are other ways—by
which to practice self-denial and self-mastery. Look
within: and many faults and failings you will see.

Giving up a grievance when you've had an unfair deal—
takes more strength of will than to deny yourself a meal
. . . Refraining from reprisals when to hit back would
be sweet—demands a greater sacrifice than missing
Friday's meat.

There are many luxuries to give up during Lent. Things
on which a lot of precious time in life is spent . . .
Now's the time to fight your demons. Now's the time to
win—the hardest fight of all against the enemies within.

Holy Week

At the gate of Easter week spare an hour or two—to ask
yourself the question, what it really means to you . . .
Turn aside from all the froth of unreality—and contem-
plate in quietness this holy mystery.

Do not say it holds no meaning for these times of strife.
More than ever do we need to hear the Word of Life . . .
Man is doomed unless he finds the Truth that sets him
free—Lost indeed without the Love revealed on Calvary.

The Challenge of the Cross

Easter brings you face to face with Christianity. Easter brings you to the meaning of the mystery. The crossroads of decision, to accept or to deny. To enthrone Him in your heart, to praise or crucify.

Easter brings you to a table in an Upper Room—to a cross upon a hill—and to an empty tomb. Easter brings you to the point where you must stand and say—Yes or No to Christ; to give assent or turn away. Easter brings the challenge of the Cross of Calvary. Life or Death, the choice before you. Which is it to be?

The Comfort of the Cross

Life without a living faith may run on smooth and bright—but there comes a day to all when sorrows dim the light . . . Then where can you look for hope? What comfort can there be—outside the circle of the Love declared on Calvary?

The Love that shines for all to see around the Easter Cross. You can pass unheeding to your everlasting loss—or taking what it offers you, redemption and release—you can find the inner glory: life and joy and peace.

The Faithful Few

Above the fears and tears and troubles of humanity, the Easter Cross is lifted up for every man to see. This, the symbol of the Love that came to meet our need. This, the message and the meaning of the Christian creed.

Nail and hammer could not kill the Love that burned within—the heart of Him in whom there was no hatred and no sin. When upon the Roman cross the wounded Hands were laid—the price demanded of that Love was well and truly paid.

Through the noonday darkness as the tortured saviour died—the faithful few remained to keep their vigil at His side. And so today; the faithful few stand by to watch and pray—waiting for the risen Christ; the Lord of Easter Day.

April

A New Lease of Life

A new lease of life is granted to the trees at winter's going. See in garden, park and lane the fresh new sap is flowing. This the law in Nature's kingdom; leases are renewed. Year by year without a break the bare boughs are endued—with the power of strength restored from root to tip again—thrilling with vitality in fibre, leaf and vein.

A new lease of life we too desire when youth has lost its rapture. April beauty and its bloom in vain we would recapture – but unlike the stricken branch that spring's light touch revives—Time is in control and measures out our little lives . . . Only in the country of the mind can we enjoy—the happiness perennial that nothing can destroy.

Another Lovely Day

With the first grey streak of light a bird begins to sing—
waking me as if to say "Get up you lazy thing—can't
you see the rising sun has chased the stars away—and
that God is sending you another lovely day."

"There you lie, though problems press and there is much
to do, but I have a nest to build. Oh yes, I'm busy too!
And my food to find, for it's the early bird that wins. Yet
I've time to sing to God before the day begins."

APRIL 3RD

Every Spring Is New

I knew it was all going to happen again: the wallflowers
aglow in the bright April rain, the violets quivering under
the hedge, the primroses clustering at the wood's edge.

Daffodils dancing in the garden and park. Rapture of birdsong from dawn until dark. Green waves advancing as
fresh leaves unfold—purple and emerald, coral and gold.

Blossom of apple, pear, cherry and plum. I knew, yes I
knew that it all had to come—but now that the magic is
working once more, it seems that it never so happened
before . . . And when you think of it, isn't it true? This
spring is different. This spring is new.

Blossomtide

It is blossomtide again . . . In the sunshine and the
rain—thrushes sing a madrigal—for the happy festival.

From the bare bough there has come—milk-white
bloom of pear and plum . . . And upon the apple tree—
pink buds cluster daintily.

Spring's green banners are unfurled. Joy comes back
into the world . . . Man may weep, but with one
voice—Nature says, "Rejoice, rejoice!"

APRIL 5TH

As God Sends Spring . . .

As God sends Spring at winter's end, and birds return
to build again—As dark woods quicken into green
beneath the kiss of April's rain—So I shall wake one
happy day and feel the pulse of life anew—Looking out
with fearless eyes upon a broader, brighter view.

Discovering forgotten dreams; the things of peace so
long denied—Learning how to live again by so many
sorrows purified . . . As new sap rises in the bough and
bursts the folded buds apart—so will hope bring forth
its flowers, and joy return unto the heart.

That Second Chance

Every night that closes a day brings opportunity—to
repent of the mistakes you made, and failed to see . . .
At the time caught up in the confusions of the day—But
now at last comes the quiet moment when you can
pause to pray—for the second chance you want to do
the thing that's right—feeling guilty you run in thought
towards tomorrow's light.

We do not deserve that second chance, nor do we ever
earn—the wages of our blessings. On we go but never
learn—On we go still grasping out for what we think
we need. Greedy for the gains of life . . . Ears deaf when
others plead—For what you could supply . . . Night
comes once more. Pay what you owe—Try again—then
into tomorrow you can safely go.

Wild Violets

Where the Winter has retreated from the nooks in copse and brake, a call goes ringing through the woods—and April violets wake.

Dyed in shades of royal purple—yet a modest flower, and shy—In some corner, unobserved, content to live and die.

There are many souls like this who love to serve in humble ways—working out their quiet purpose—seeking neither fame nor praise.

APRIL 8TH

The Scene Changes

The hedge, once black like twisted iron, is now enlaced with tender leaves—Green of budding honeysuckle foams about the cottage eaves . . . In the orchard overnight, a mist has come: a rosy haze— where the swelling apple bloom is breaking on the clustered sprays.

The scene is changing every day. New beauties burst upon our sight. The trees, once dark against the sky, are caught in threads of golden light . . . Outlines soften; colours deepen, in the sunshine and the rain. A miracle is happening; the world is being born again.

April Rain

Under the kiss of the April rain—the old earth comes alive again—young and fresh and beautiful—decked as for a carnival . . . The blossoms thicken on the spray. The hedges quicken by the way. A primrose tapestry is spread—on laneside bank and garden bed.

The earth's old face that bore the sign—of winter's frown is now ashine—with smiles that radiate a glow—where daffodils and lilacs blow—and wallflowers by the path unfold—yellow, amber, red and gold.

In the dawn the bird choirs rise—anthems of ecstatic praise. In the heart joy leaps anew. The dream of spring has all come true—for under the kiss of the April rain—the tired old earth is young again.

So Little

The gentle smile, the reconciling touch—can cost so little
and can mean so much—to heal a breach or mend a
friendship broken—a letter written, or a sentence spoken.

What hurts and pangs we suffer needlessly! What pains
inflict, because we cannot see—how much we lose
through conflicts and contentions—poisoning life with
quarrels and dissensions.

Let them all go and love triumphant be—over all evil,
hate, greed, jealousy . . . Love's tender word, forbearing
and forgiving—brings to the heart true peace and joy
 of living.

A Farmer's Dream

Beyond the ridges of the hills the bright green valleys lie—Rich with promise for the future; pleasant to the eye . . . The ploughman ploughs his furrows and the sower sows his seeds, and healthy herds graze peacefully about the watermeads.

The orchards foam with blossom and the flocks feed by the stream. Is this England, born again? . . . Or just a farmer's dream? We cannot tell until we've climbed the rough and rugged slope—Beyond those storm-crowned hills where lies the country of our hope.

April Day

Many an exile far away is thinking of an English lane. Many a homesick heart to-day remembers with a stab of pain—Blackthorn wet with April rain; a row of elms; the sound of rooks. Primrose banks and hazel hedges; violets by the wayside brooks.

Down the path of Memory the dreamer wanders and he sees—daffodils in cottage gardens; blossom on the lilac trees . . . England beckons to her children—calls them home from far away, when her lanes are at their fairest on a lovely April day.

Down in the Secret Garden

Year by year the blackbird comes the April nest to
build. Year by year the little sunken garden here is
filled—with liquid notes that rise and fall like fountains
through the trees—in a jet of silvery music blowing on
the breeze.

Deep below the street it lies, this narrow walled-in
place—and upon the moss green stones the shadows
interlace—when boughs of apple and of lilac in the
wind are stirred . . . Year by year it comes, the magic
fluting of this bird—down there in the secret garden
somewhere out of sight—in the morning glory and the
mellow evening light.

How Can You?

How can you cling to a grief that is old—when blossoms are breaking all rosy and gold . . . How can you hold to a sad old regret—when Nature is saying, rejoice and forget.

How can you brood over things that went wrong—when outside the window a thrush makes a song? How can you think of ill luck or mischance—when down in the orchard the daffodils dance?

How can you fail to be glad in your heart—when new buds are swelling and bursting apart . . . How can you sit there and not want to sing—your praise to the Lord for the joy of Spring.

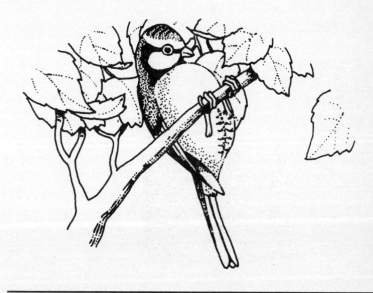

Green Dust

There is green dust sprinkled on the hedges in the lane—Green dust spangled with the glitter of the morning rain . . . Little tender leaves uncurling on each sprig and spray. Tips of shoots and new buds bursting all along the way.

Magic dust! . . . The sign of life, renewal and rebirth—Formed out of a secret force in air and sun and earth—Settling on the bushes and the branches of the trees. Green dust blowing round the world upon the April breeze.

Facets

To get at the secrets of God the Creator—we seek and we pry and we probe—Unmoved by the thought that in touching a petal—we finger the hem of His robe.

We sift and examine the dust of the stars—to discover fresh worlds in the blue . . . Forgetting that here, with the breath of each morning—the world is created anew.

We think we are clever and boast of our brains—only when some gem of new knowledge we find . . . But it's only a facet reflecting the glory—of God and His Infinite Mind.

Heritage

Leave us a few little copses. Do not sweep them all away—where the primroses bloom in April and the bluebells come out in May. Leave us the woods and the meadows where the children can climb and play and get to know God's small creatures, learning the natural way.

Leave us a few little corners, where the leafy pathways wind, for we need what the trees can give us: health and healing and peace of mind. Leave us our unspoilt village—with its church and cricket green—for history lies in the beauty of this quiet English scene.

Wherever the good land is threatened, resist, protest, complain. Build round the towns if it's needed, but leave us the country lane. The pastures the fields and the orchards. The earth that supplies what we need. The country is ours for keeping: a heritage precious indeed.

Once Again

Once again the apple blossom hangs above the garden walls—and upon the evening air the scent is borne, and sweetness falls—drifting through the open windows, fresh and fragrant after rain. Year by year with every spring we say, "The old tree lives again".

Now across the weeping world the splendour of the sunset streams—gilding every wet green leaf. Through tangled boughs the gold light gleams . . . A thrush amongst the topmost branches, perched upon a dripping flower—sings a song of purest rapture for the glory of the hour.

Month of Rainbows

April is the month of rainbows: sunshine after rain.
April comes to tell us that in spite of strife and pain—
Joy is ever waiting at the threshold of the heart. Life has
always something good and lovely to impart.

April comes to give us lessons in philosophy—When the
day is dark and stormy, suddenly we see—silver edges to
the linings of the skies of grey—in a moment it is light,
a bright and sunny day.

Rainbows spanning earth and heaven: promise of
new hope—In the presence of such glory, dare we
grieve or mope?

Is not this the hand of God upon the cloud above: the
symbol of His covenant of mercy and of love.

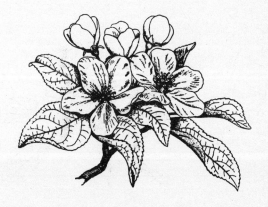

Listen!

'Listen'—that's a lovely word—it makes us quiet and
still. There's so much in the world to hear: the birds that
chirp and trill; the wild wind fluting in the trees; the
drumming of the rain the muffled fluttering of moths
against a window pane: Chopin, Beethoven,
Liszt and Grieg—giants of music's art created golden
melodies to stir the human heart.

The world is full of lovely sounds—they fall about our
ears. Remembered in serenity, they echo down the years:
a voice we loved, a waterfall, a violin, a thrush, all steal
into the quiet heart in Memory's solemn hush . . . So
close your eyes and listen, you will hear all kinds of
things—the secret language of the flowers, the whirr
of fairies wings . . .

The Carnival

The nation may be burdened by a load of dreary care—
but Nature takes no notice of disaster or despair—She
continues unconcerned her carnival of bloom. What is it
to her—this talk of deficit and doom?

Nature's mood is happy, reckless, generous and gay.
The air is filled with birdsong from the dawn till close
of day . . . Nature decks the trees with blossom,
crimson, pink and white—scattering her riches in a
frenzy of delight.

God is in His Heaven sing the birds from leafy towers.
Everything is young again proclaim the bursting flowers
. . . Man alone is sunk in gloom with no good news
to tell—while God's other creatures are declaring—
All is well.

Not Easy

It's not always easy to hold your tongue when people
   are unkind.
It's not always easy to walk away and put it from your
   mind—
but quarrelling never put anything right, it seems to
   make things worse,
and leaves you with a hornet's nest of grievances to
   nurse.

It's not always easy to turn aside and show the other
   cheek,
because you're afraid they will think that you are
   spiritless and weak . . .
No, it's not easy but it's the only thing to do you'll
   find—
if you want to keep your friendships and your peace of
   mind.

Where Shakespeare Walked

Brighter blows the cowslip in the fields where Shakespeare strayed. Sweeter grows the primrose in the fairy-haunted glade. And lovelier over Shottery the April sunlight gleams, where Shakespeare walked and wove the stuff of his immortal dreams. The bells that peal through Stratford town with golden clappers swing.

And birds by Avon's bank with a diviner rapture sing, because great Shakespeare here was born to add to England's fame. The riches of his genius, the glory of his name.

APRIL 24TH

The Living Picture

The pear tree leaning to the window now is robed in bridal white. The twisted boughs are netted thickly in a mesh golden light . . . And in the foam of creamy flowers, a blackbird dark as ebony—sits and floods the evening garden with his April melody.

Through the long grey days of winter I have dreamed this dream of Spring. I have waited for this wonder: bursting bud and beating wing . . . Now I see a living picture at the casement of my room: throbbing throat and flowering branches; glossy breast and snowy bloom.

Not All Plain Sailing

Life cannot be all plain sailing—that calls for no effort from you. Just drifting in summery weather with never a cloud in the blue.

You never can tell in the morning what sort of day it will be. Although it begins in calm waters, a storm may blow up suddenly, to land you in all kinds of trouble. So know how to handle your sails—gliding along in the sunshine or steering a course through the gales. Ready for changing direction, unruffled when put to the test, by failure, success or misfortune. Prepared for the worst and the best.

Over the Gate

If between the apple orchards up the hill you go—you will find a gate that's chained and locked—and rightly so . . . Climb it. None will question if you've come just for the joy of seeing bluebells, not to pick, to plunder or destroy.

Once you're over, dumb you're struck and spellbound there you stand. The gate that looked forbidding was the gate to fairyland . . . Half afraid, you hesitate. It's all so still and strange—that lake of blueness flowing out as far as eye can range.

The path I've often wandered but the end I've never found—for I felt a Presence there and it was holy ground. Not for me this ecstasy. I'd come back later on—when the blue had faded and the mystery had gone.

Moods

April keeps us guessing with her sunshine and her showers. In the wake of storms she brings the rainbow and the flowers. First she smiles a radiant smile and then she frowns and broods. It is hard to keep up with her ever-changing moods.

Do not be like April, one day bright, the next in tears, Always at the mercy of your moods, your hopes and fears . . . Live life in the sunshine of a gay philosophy One that does not vary with the winds of destiny.

Thankfulness

Look back in thankfulness and you'll admit life wasn't so bad after all. You've had your troubles like everyone else but honestly, if you recall the joy and the sorrow, the good and the bad, and weigh it all up in your mind, you, if you're truthful, will have to confess that Time was not wholly unkind.

Look back in thankfulness and you will say that there was more pleasure than pain. More blessings than crosses; look back and you'll see—that there was more sunshine than rain.

Snow in the Orchard

In the orchard snow has fallen—Every spray is wintry white—Just as if some fairy wand had touched the branches overnight . . . Not the snows of cold December, but the magic snows of Spring—Boughs of apple, pear and cherry gay with April's blossoming.

Soon, too soon, the thaw will come—like snowflakes melting in the sun—The flowers will fade, the glory pass, the petals wither, one by one . . . But underneath the snows of blossom waits the green and tender shoot—with the promise of fulfilment—bud and blossom, flower and fruit.

APRIL 30TH

This Their Legacy

Build up not out if build you must—and spare the countryside—for this is England's heritage and this is England's pride! The primrose lanes of April and the bluebell woods of May. The pastures bright with buttercups, the banks and hedges gay—with roses and with honeysuckle, thorn and gorse and broom: the meadows and the cliffside paths where honeyed heathers bloom . . . Hold these things in trust for generations yet to be. Keep them for our children's children. This their legacy.

May

This Lovely World

Once again the lilac tassels flutter in the breeze—and the green leaves open out upon the budding trees. There are new lambs in the field and fledglings in the nest—as the old earth wakes once more out of its winter rest.

In the orchards blossom breaks in white and rosy spray. Gardens, parks and cottage plots are glorious and gay—with beds of tulips, pink and scarlet blazing rich and bold—and wallflowers massed in glowing shades of amber, wine and gold.

In the woods the bluebells make a carpet thick and bright. The hawthorns in the hedges are bedecked in bridal white—and the yellow banners of laburnums are unfurled . . . How thankful we should be for this our good and lovely world!

Green Curtains

Nature hangs green curtains round the edges so
that we—shan't probe into secrets that are hidden
cunningly—amongst the closely clustered twigs away
from prying eyes—And thus she guards against assault,
rough touch and rude surprise.

Behind the leafy lattice there are busy flutterings—
From the thicket comes the quiver of protective
wings . . . The ageless drama of creation goes on year
by year—and soon from out the hidden nest the new
life will appear.

MAY 3RD

The Instrument

Play life like an instrument making melodies. Change
the daily discords into harmonies. . . Draw the sweetness from it. Somebody may hear—the tune behind the
strident sounds that jar upon the ear. Make your music
as you move through the world's distress—Someone
passing by may catch your note of happiness . . . Play
life gently play it softly. Play with style and grace—
bringing beauty out of what is dull and commonplace.

Spring

Only a God with a thinking mind could have thought up the joys of Spring—tinting the grass with an emerald dye and teaching the birds to sing—covering hazels with powdery tassels that shimmer in every breeze—spraying the almonds with rosy pink petals and hanging the cherry trees—with bridal-white blossom, and staining the copses with patches of flowers growing wild: celandines, violets, bluebells and primroses, lovely and undefiled.

Only a God with a loving heart could have made us a world like this—where you wake up one morning and find the air as soft and as warm as a kiss—A world where like magic the daffodils come with their trumpets all glowing and bright—as if He repeated the Genesis fiat and said again, Let there be light . . . Blind evolution could not of itself have created a butterfly's wing—Only a God could have ever designed it—so praise Him, the God of the Spring.

Nature's Wonderland

For all our vaunted cleverness we cannot understand
The beauty and the mystery of Nature's wonderland.
The sun, the moon, the whirling stars, the sea, the sky,
   the earth—
All the many miracles of life and death and birth.

Man with marvellous machines can do stupendous
   things
But could not with his hands create a bird with voice
   and wings.
Could not make a rose, rainbow, or a common weed,
A chrysalis, a dragonfly, a cabbage or a seed.

Cannot say what magic holds the planet in its place
Or how the spider spins its dainty web of fairy lace . . .
He cannot make a blade of grass, a leaf, a cone, a pod
Yet he is too arrogant to give the praise to God.

London Gardens

London is a mighty maze—of busy roads and crowded ways. For miles and miles the pavements go—And yet the dingy streets can show—more loveliness of bloom and green—than any I have ever seen.

In spite of smoke and dust and grime—How London smiles in blossom time! . . . Laburnum, lilac, chestnut, may. So fair she looks, so young and gay. Her gardens fresh and beautiful—bedecked as if for carnival.

MAY 7TH

Joy Unfading

Bored we grow with science, its inventions and its powers—but never do we take for granted birds and trees and flowers. Never do we tire of seeing hawthorn in the lane, blossom on the apple bough and lilacs in the rain.

Never grow too old to feel a thrill that's ever new, when the nightingales arrive and when the woods are blue—with bluebells spread in fairy carpets down the leafy glades. The heart responds to these, God's gifts, with joy that never fades.

All Our Days Are Numbered

All our days are numbered but it's not for us to know—
just how many days are left. So don't let this one go—
unmarked by something good or lovely, something
true or fine—something that redeems it with a touch
of the divine.

Think a thought that lifts your mind on to a higher
track. Do the thing that takes a load from someone
else's back . . . Say the word that changes conflict
into harmony. Strike the note that turns the discord
into melody.

Take this day out of its groove. Before you let it go—
give to it a meaning and a glory. Let it glow! There are
many little ways in which it's possible—to sanctify the
commonplace and make it beautiful.

Not for You

Let the bluebell ring and swing upon its sturdy stem.
Let them blow beneath the trees just where God
planted them.

Let them live! . . . and give to all who love the countryside—the joy of walking in the woodlands when the
earth is dyed—in lovely hues of heavenly blues—flower-
carpets bright and thick.

. . . Leave them please just where they are. They're
NOT FOR YOU TO PICK!

Home

I try to make my home a place that's beautiful to see,
to fill each room with lovely things—and perfect
   harmony,
to polish up the copper pots, the silver and the brass,
and rub the walnut table till it gleams like crystal glass . . .
But home is not mere furniture.
The objects we see here are visible expressions of a
   wonderful Idea—
a power that draws with ties of love wherever we may
   roam.
The centre of the universe and of the heart—the Home.

Lilac Days

They say that it's unlucky to pick the lilac bloom, but what can be more lovely than lilac in a room? Filling it with sweetness and scenting every space. Touching with a magic things dull and commonplace.

How can it be unlucky? What evil can it bring? The smell of it is heaven—the very breath of Spring . . . It follows and precedes you. It lingers everywhere. It steals into the corner and clings about the stair.

Too soon, too soon it withers; a sad and sorry sight. The deepest richest purple, the purest waxy white . . . So gather for your pleasure the longest brightest sprays. So transient is the beauty. So brief the lilac days.

The Best in Life

The best and sweetest things in life are things you
   cannot buy:
the music of the birds at dawn, the rainbows in the sky;
the dazzling magic of the stars, the miracle of the light;
the precious gifts of health and strength, of hearing,
   speech and sight;

the peace of mind that crowns a busy
life of work well done; a faith in God
that deepens as you face the setting sun;
the pearl of love, the gems of friendship.
As the years go by
you find the greatest blessings are the things you
   cannot buy.

Hawthorn

The wind is sweetened by the breath of white and crimson may. Fragrant is the evening breeze that fans the flowering spray. Little lanes lie deep in shadow where the hedges rise—making solid walls of blossom, high against the skies.

Just a few months ago these thorns were black and bare—Hard as iron like beaten metal in the frosty air . . . Now their leafy bowers conceal new life and hidden wings—Offering sanctuary to furred and feathered things.

Look at Me

"Look at me," says the tulip, "if you are feeling low—
discouraged or disgruntled, and life has lost its glow . . .
Be like me," says the tulip, "lift up your empty cup—
waiting for the sunshine to come and fill it up."

"Look at me," says the tulip. "Stand calm and straight
and strong—unruffled and unbroken when rough winds
blow along . . . You, too, are God's creation.
You, too, are wonderful. A human, like a flower, is a
living miracle."

"I live to make life lovely for all who come my way. I
do not strive or struggle, but quietly day by day—I
grow within the compass of the plan ordained for me:
to adorn the corner where I was meant to be."

When God Sends a Beautiful Day

Somehow the world seems a wonderful place.
There's an excitement that quickens the pace . . .
Suddenly everyone's smiling and gay—When God sends
a beautiful day.

You cannot explain it, you do not know why—but
things look quite different when from the sky—the sun
in its glory from Heaven looks down—pouring its
blessings on country and town.

The troubles that yesterday weighed on your mind—
seem unimportant. You leave them behind . . . The
future looks bright and your cares melt away—when
God sends a beautiful day.

There in Spirit

Now the bright-eyed daisies open, and the buttercups
unfold—spreading on the watermeads a dazzling cloth
of purest gold . . . White clouds sail the blue of heaven;
white herds graze beside the stream . . . Far from home,
yet there in spirit—I, in exile, dream this dream.

In my fancy I am leaning on the old gate in the lane—
seeing Maytime come to England, and the fields turn
gold again—Gazing at the yellow pastures where the
silver waters thread—Listening with the old sweet
wonder to a skylark overhead.

MAY 17TH

Song in the Blue

Somewhere in the depths of space beyond the range of
sight—an unseen bird is singing in a rapture of delight
. . . Like a shower of golden rain the notes of ecstasy—
flood the heavens and the earth with sweetest melody.

Where I wonder did the skylark learn his magic art—
He can move the soul to tears and heal a broken heart
. . . God created us for Joy. We feel it must be true—
when we hear His little minstrels singing in the blue.

Falling Petals

At the point where spring and summer meet—petals fall in showers about your feet. From apple, damson, cherry, plum and pear—they flutter like confetti through the air—making fairy rings upon the grass, that widen as the gentle breezes pass.

And as you watch the stripping of the tree—you feel regret that it should have to be. It looked so lovely but a week ago—crowned with bloom. But in your heart you know—that there would be no time of harvesting unless the blossom perished with the spring. Where it has fallen, withered, faded, dead—ripe fruited boughs will soon be thickly spread.

Seed Bed

A nursery of unborn life, where seeds as dry as dust— quicken in their secret cells and through the darkness thrust—their tender shoots of living green into the open air—blooming slowly into something marvellously fair.

Marigolds and hollyhocks and poppies flaming red— will spring as if by magic from this little narrow bed . . . Pansies, cornflowers, mignonette and lupins bright and gay—All the beauty and the glory of a summer's day.

Just Kindness

Kindness, just kindness is all that it takes—to make a day happy, for kindliness makes—for peace and for cheerfulness, grace and goodwill—stirring no trouble, and speaking no ill.

Feeling for others and trying to ease—the burden that presses, to help and to please—forgetting yourself and your own heavy load—thinking of somebody else on the road.

The value of kindness you cannot assess. Spoken or written no word can express—how one little kindness can make someone's day—giving him courage to go on his way—a smile on his lips and a song in his mind—just because somebody somewhere was kind.

The Field Path

Across the golden field it runs—now bright with butter-cups of May—between the grasses, thick and green—it makes its own haphazard way—and climbs the hill with leisured pace—to where the church, triumphant stands—Looking out across the sweep of rich and rolling pasture-lands.

Folk throughout the countless years have worn the earth into a path—coming from the distant farms, from castle gate and cottage hearth—Have left in white and wintry days their footprints in the driven snow—and now they tread the flowery track where daisies bloom and cowslips blow.

MAY 22ND

Tell Me

Tell me how a seagull glides with such an easy grace. Tell me, how do migrants through the trackless heavens trace—a path above the seas and mountains with their tiny wings? Tell me how a nest is built and why a sky-lark sings. Tell me how a blossom bursts out of a leafless tree. Tell me how the earth revolves, for it's a mystery . . . Tell me what puts life into the beating heart of a man—and how the power of love can change it. Tell me if you can.

Troubles Never Last

Don't assume that life will be all May days. Make a
plan for coping with the grey days—so that when they
come—as come they will, you will be prepared. You'll
know the drill. Have a grey day programme all worked
out. Smile up at the cloud and never doubt—that
behind the smoky murky smear—there's glory . . . All is
sunshine. All is clear.

This remember always. Don't be caught—off your
guard. Be ready with a thought—that warms the heart.
Though skies be overcast—Troubles, like bad weather,
never last.

MAY 24TH

Polyanthus

Like an oriental carpet laid along the border bed.
Worked in deeply glowing colours thickly planted,
richly spread. Polyanthus in the sunshine gay and
gorgeous, bright and bold. Claret red and butter
yellow, tangerine and honey gold. Feast your eyes
upon the splendour so when come the winter hours—
you will see on memory's screen the living carpet of
the flowers . . . Why must all this beauty wither and
the glory fade away? Oh that it would linger longer,
this most lovely month of May!

Every Day, Every Year

You need every friend you can make—in a world where things hurt, and hearts break. Friends who will always be there—the good and the bad times to share . . . But friendship two-sided must be—each giving much, yet both free—going a separate way—wherever life leads day by day.

Friendships, the new and the old—forms links that connect and will hold—in spite of the day to day strain—One friendship will always remain . . . Through changes and chances you learn—To this one special friend you can turn—the friend who unchanged will appear any time—any day—any year.

MAY 26TH

The Little Fir

Year by year the little fir strains up into the blue— putting out its fresh green growth of needles, bright and new . . . Thrusting up its strong young arms towards the golden light—Growing slowly all the time in strength and girth and height.

Learning all the secrets of the wind's wild gossiping— Giving hospitality to birds upon the wing . . . Reaching sunward; pushing upward; climbing steadily—to the full and final glory of maturity.

The Key Word

Do not think that happiness resides in just what you
possess. Seek that happiness within—and every morning
will begin—with thoughts of joy and gratitude—
Cultivate the attitude—that life is sweet and life is
good—if God's great laws are understood.

Do not say you cannot see—the glimpses of divinity—
behind the drab and commonplace—you feel the everlasting grace—but only with your inner sight—can you
perceive this hidden light; this aura, making dull things
shine—with splendour from a source benign.

In the crowds that throng the street—a radiant face you
seldom meet—so marked they are with lines of care.
A sunny countenance is rare . . . The world with all its
sham and show—can't tell you what you long to know:
the key word that will heal and bless . . . The secret of
true happiness.

Trees

What would life be like without the trees—with no green leaf to quiver in the breeze—To cast a cooling shadow on the grass—and mark the changing seasons as they pass? Imagine towns with no old tree to spread—a canopy of branches overhead: a tree with boughs outstretched towards the sky—as if to bless the people rushing by.

MAY 29TH

Take a Little Time

Take a little time for seeing—grass and blooms with dew impearled—Take a little time for being – Quiet in your own small world . . . Take a little time for sowing—flowers amongst life's many weeds—Some day you will see them glowing—growing from the hidden seeds. Take a little time to ponder—what is in your secret heart—Take a little time to wander—in the silence set apart . . . Take a little time for living—busy though your day may be—Take a little time for giving—happiness to somebody.

Wild Forget-me-nots

When bees hum in the linden tree and roses bloom
in cottage plots.
Along the brookside banks we see the blue of wild
  forget-me-nots.
Shy flowers that shun the prying eye—content to let
  the daisy hold,
The glances of the passers-by with brazen stare of
  white and gold.
Forget-me-not! From long ago it stirs the thought of
  happier days.
For memories like wild flowers grow—along the heart's
  untrodden ways.

Trying to Read

How can I think about serious things—when the air is
alive with the flutter of wings? How can I focus my
mind on this book—when the happy nonsensical song
of a brook, scatters my thoughts to the wind?—So why
try—to cope with a subject so dull and so dry?

How can I concentrate, grave and subdued—when
Nature is in this hilarious mood—and laughs in my face
with the wind and the sun—as if to say, "Come on, and
join in the fun?
Don't be a sobersides—solemn and glum . . . God's in
His Heaven, and Summer has come."

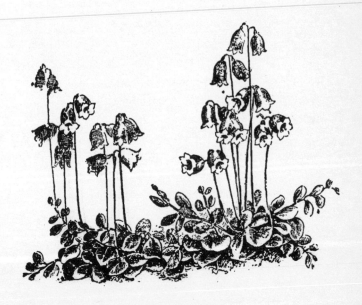

June

Roses Everywhere

Here again comes lovely June! No place on earth can
  show
Such beauty as our Britain in the summer's early glow.
Washed by softly falling rains the grass grows greener
  here
And where else on this globe does Heaven seem to be
  so near?

Carpeted with buttercups the golden meadows blaze.
Wild flowers flow along the verges of the country ways.
Bright is every cottage garden in the winding lanes
With jasmine and with honeysuckle at the windowpanes.
Gardens bright with candy-tuft, with thrift and irises.
Pathways edged with lupins, pansies, pinks and peonies.
Stocks in rainbow tinges that cast their sweetness on
  the air.
And roses white, pink, gold and crimson. Roses
  everywhere.

The Happy Life

All men seek the happy life; down many roads they fare,
Searching for a pleasant path away from strife and care,
Looking for some hidden turning where the sunlight
   gleams,
Following their star of fortune down the track of
   dreams.

Restless, never satisfied, life's winding ways they wend,
Always thinking there'll be something better round the
   bend—
Pressing on towards some distant castle in the blue,
Never pausing where they stand, the present scene to
   view.

Learn to live each passing day as if it were the last:
Do not dwell in thought upon the future or the past.
It is good to dream a dream; it helps you on your
   way—
But remember you can live the happy life. . . Today.

That's Why God Made Flowers

Flowers can speak the language of the heart. Flowers a
quiet message can impart . . . Love's most secret
thoughts they can convey—telling what no lips can
ever say.

Flowers can heal a hurt and flowers can bless – giving
comfort, hope and happiness . . . Flowers perform a
silent ministry—bringing peace, affection, sympathy.

There are things that cannot be confessed. Things that
go too deep to be expressed—by tongue or pen in life's
most poignant hours—of joy or sorrow. That's why God
made flowers.

JUNE 4TH

Fantasy

The clouds are like a fleet of ships with canvas spreading wide—rolling on the rosy billows of the sunset tide.
. . From my little window I can see them moving by—
out upon the golden ocean of the evening sky.

Darkness falls, and slowly now the dim shapes drift
away—deep into the purple distance, lost in starry spray
. . . Sailing on the ebbing ripples of the fading light—
Vanishing beyond the far horizons of the night.

The Mill Stream

By the mill the little stream goes peacefully upon its
way. Willows stoop upon the bank where swallows
skim and children play . . . Through a thick bright lace
of leaves the dappled gold of sunlight falls—where the
swan glides in the shadow of the ivy-covered walls.

Once the stream rushed, loud and busy, past this latticed
window pane—Full of froth and self-importance,
turning wheels and grinding grain . . . Now unhurriedly
it flows where green boughs trail amongst the reeds—
slowly, softly slipping out into the quiet water-meads.

A Glimpse of England

Water-meadows rich and green where herds of cattle
 graze.
An old stone bridge round which there clings a dream
 of bygone days . . .
Streams where pollard willows stoop and graceful
 swans glide by.
Pools that hold the lights and shadows of the changing sky.

Across the fields the Minster towers rise up as if to crown
The quaint old streets and houses of the little market-town.
This is what we fought for! For this we shall hold fast.
The beauty that is England—and the glory of the Past.

The Coming Day

I shan't go rushing through the coming day—at full stretch all the while and all the way although a busy day it's going to be—I'll take my time to do things thoroughly.

. . . I'll set my pace, yet not a moment waste— squandering my strength by frantic haste—and feeling tired before the day has gone—conserving power . . . Just plodding quietly on.

If I Get to Heaven

If ever by God's mercy I should find myself in Heaven— with all my failings overlooked and all my sins for-given—I hope there'll be a little plot where I can grow some flowers. What better way could I employ the everlasting hours?

I cannot see why such a hope should seem impossible— for did not God prepare an Eden green and beautiful—to be the scene of creation of the soul of man? Amidst the flowers and birds and trees was where the world began . . . So, Lord, if I get to Heaven having won Thy pardon—I'll turn a patch of paradise into an English garden.

Live Out Your Dreams

Happy you looked on that wonderful day—when you walked down the aisle with your bridal bouquet—But did you, by any chance, hear someone say—it would be roses and cream all the way? . . . Of course not; you ought to have known then and there—that marriage means learning to build and to share—working at making your home a success—giving and taking; that's life . . . more or less.

And here you are wishing you two hadn't met. What did you think you were going to get—Heaven on earth without passing the test? Run home, and weigh up the worst with the best. Bury the grievance—your promise renew. Live out your dream and our dream will come true.

The Crimson Tapestry

I thought the climber planted by the wall would never thrive. The first year and the second year it hardly kept alive—beyond a tiny leaf or two, but when the third year came—it burst into a blaze of life with buds of fiery flame—that opened in the sun. Now year by year the rich blooms glow—against the russet-tinted bricks . . . which only goes to show that Nature takes her time. Below the ground the roots are spread—and just when you are thinking that the thing is nearly dead—she springs a wonderful surprise! Now every June I see—the old wall hidden underneath a crimson tapestry, a tapestry of roses where amongst the green and red—the sunshine works a shining pattern with a golden thread.

Forgotten Trails

You'd hardly notice it at all, this green and narrow lane—and yet it must have known the tread of Saxon and of Dane . . . Before the Romans, Britons must have hunted in this glade. On these hills men lived and loved and little children played.

It's just a rose-hedged path between the village and the sea—And yet it runs right back into the dawn of history . . . Time has left its footprint on our downs and plains and vales—We read our ancient story in these old forgotten trails.

Walking Pace

If feet could go as fast as wheels, a pity it would be—
because you'd move so quickly that you'd never really
see—the wild rose by the wayside and the cloudscapes
in the sky. All the things that go unnoticed when you're
rushing by.

Butterflies and dragonflies and shadows cast by trees . . .
snowy flakes of falling blossom drifting on the breeze.
Bees with golden pollen flecked . . . the flashing of a
wing. Thistledown and gossamer and rushes quivering.

Ducks on ponds and little creatures by the road's green
edge. Bead eyes peeping shyly from the shelter of the
hedge. Raindrops glinting diamond-bright on stalk and
leaf and flower . . . what a lot we miss when we exceed
four miles an hour!

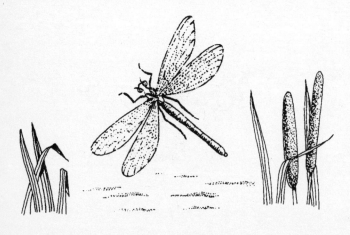

Upside Down

Upside down and inside out this mad world seems today—When you come to think of it you know not what to say—Are we crazy rushing on along the road to doom—never caring where we're going, never making room – for sober thoughts that lead away from never-ending strife—towards the pastures of a more enlightened mode of life.

Did no-one ever warn us and has no-one ever heard—the voice that in the silence speaks the Everlasting Word?—Blind and deaf and ignorant, this voice we failed to heed—pathetic now we stand unguarded in our hour of need—clutching at a reed to keep afloat and keep alive—the Bible to restore, to resurrect and to revive.

Colouring

Colours make the beauty of the earth and of the sky.
Grass-green meadows, clay-brown land and white
clouds floating by. Golden dawns and rosy sunsets and
the lovely tones—of colourings in gems and jewels,
shells and rocks and stones.

Garden flowers and country flowers in varied rainbow
hues: pinks and purples, grey and silver, lavenders and
blues . . . What are colours? How would you define
them to the blind, so that they imagining, could see
them in the mind? Yellow corn and wine–dark rose, a
butterfly's bright wing. How could you explain in words
this thing called colouring?

The Hay Wagon

Along the deep sun-dappled lane with hedges green
and gay—there comes a horse and wagon with a load
of fragrant hay . . . Through the farmyard gates it goes,
along the rutted tracks—to the field where sun-tanned
men are busy on the stacks.

To and fro it goes between the meadow and the farm—a
scene of peace, of simple beauty and of rustic charm . . . A
scene that lingers in the heart and comes before the eyes—
of countrymen who dream of home beneath the city skies.

June Bride

Married in the month of roses when the year is in its
  prime,
And all Nature is rejoicing in the glow of summertime.
Married in the lovely season when the sun is high and
  bright,
When the air is sweet and fragrant and the days are
  long and light.

Happy be the bride of June, not only on her wedding
  day,
But may she have the joy we wish her all the while and
  all the way.
May she cherish in her heart this glad and glorious
  memory—
To keep the flame of love alight through the years that
  are to be.

Little Streams

There's something about a little stream that threads between the trees—something that pacifies the heart and puts the mind at ease. There's something about the sound of water with its soothing tones—lapping gently at the banks and rippling over stones—that brings a strange tranquillity relieving inner stress.

So go and find some little stream and there in quietness—seek the peace that Nature offers to the soul distraught: the peace of little streams that calms the storms of troubled thought.

JUNE 18TH

The Interruption

The fragrant silence of the night was shattered by the siren's wail. The boom of guns broke in upon the music of a nightingale . . . The stars that had been strung like lamps above the elm trees in the lane—were outshone by bursting rockets falling in a crimson rain.

The skies that should have held such peace upon this perfect night of June—became a roaring field of battle blazing round the young white moon . . . The fighters passed, the stars came back, the drone of engines died away. The nightingale took up his song and sang on 'til the break of day.

Time Is Life

You can't buy or borrow a minute. Time isn't for sale.
  Time is Life.
Yet how we squander and waste it – in worry and folly
  and strife
And things of no value or merit – the pleasures that die
  with the day.
If Time were for sale how we'd treasure the hours that
  we fritter away!

Spend Time as you spend gold or silver. Spend wisely
  what Time God may give.
Time wasted is Time gone forever. It can't be recalled to
  relive.
And when at last Time grows precious and Time is the
  thing you lack
You think of lost friends and lost chances and the days
  that will never come back.

Summer to Remember

Have something to show for the summer. The long
lovely evenings are sweet. Go work in the garden or go
take a walk in a lane or a park or a street . . . Don't sit
at a wheel or watching a screen for there's naught you
can hear or can view—half as exciting or half as delight-
ful as all that is waiting for you—out in the open where
songbirds are singing and where you can breathe in the
fresh air—making the most of the fugitive moments
whenever there's time you can spare.

Build up your health. Study Nature's own book. Learn
to love both the sun and the rain . . . Make it a
summer that you will remember when winter comes
round once again.

The Rose

I saw a rose in the morning mist through a haze of pearly light. I saw it again when its flame-red heart had opened, warm and bright . . . I noted its beauty— remembering the corner where it grew—and when you came in the starry dusk I picked that rose for you.

'Twas only a tiny episode in the chapter of the day— but as I stood at the cottage gate and watched you walk away—It seemed that there was a hidden meaning charged with destiny. So late you came. So late—Too late to share the best with me.

Too late for Love and for its flowering in the blaze of noon—the raptures and the agonies of life's flamboyant June . . . But is this not the best—this quiet bliss, untouched by tears; this afterglow of friendship in the sunset of the years?

Love Knows the Answer

Love is the answer to every question. Love is the sign-post that points the way. Love's the solution of all the problems that must be dealt with day by day.

Stand still and listen to Love's sweet counsel—when you're unsure of the choice to make. Turn a deaf ear to what self is saying. Love knows the course it is wise to take.

Follow Love's promptings in all your dealings. Love knows the best thing to do and say. Love's voice is God's voice that speaks inside you—Trust it to guide you and obey.

Summer Night

Open the window on the beauty of a summer night, and look at the sleeping garden through a veil of starry light. Silence like a benediction rests on leaf and flower. Take it deep into your soul, this peace . . . this quiet hour.

Round the sill the roses and the jasmine interlace—and like the fumes of incense rising in a holy place— fragrance from the earth is drawn and scent comes drifting up, from breath of pinks, syringa, stock and lily cup. Gather up into your mind the healing and the balm— your restless thoughts to pacify, your troubled heart to calm.

Picnic

It's fun to have a picnic on a lovely summer's day
in some green meadow where a little river winds its way;
a fragrant bank where willows trail their branches
  gracefully.
It's nice to have a party underneath a kind old tree . . .
To spread the cloth upon the grass, and set the plates
  around;
to drink your tea and eat your cakes while seated on
  the ground—
fat doughnuts, jam and creamy buns, and things that
  normally
you really wouldn't dream of eating with your cup
  of tea!
Your fingers may be sticky, but that's half the fun of it,
the wasps may settle in the jam, but you won't care a bit!

But when you've had your picnic, don't forget to make
  the place
exactly as you found it, leaving not a single trace . . .
For if, for instance, you were asked to tea with friends
  next door—
you wouldn't leave a lot of litter lying on the floor, now
  would you?
And it's just the same in Nature's lovely bowers.
She's so hospitable and kind – she gives us fields and
flowers,
and shady nooks by babbling brooks, where we can
take our ease,
and have a picnic underneath the shelter of the trees.

The Music of the Sea

There's a magic in the music of the restless sea. There's a fascination in the endless symphony—played upon the instruments of wind and wave and spray—rising in crescendo on a wild and stormy day—or dying on a quiet note beneath the moon's pale gleams. Never does the heart grow weary of the changing themes—that swell to angry tones or lull to moods of somnolence— the everlasting orchestration of the elements.

JUNE 26TH

Verges

Lovely are the verges of the lane in summertide—with Queen Ann's Lace with buttercups and daisies golden-eyed . . . making glowing patterns like a rich embroidery—laid between the hedges and the roads for all to see. . . But seldom do we stop to look as hurriedly we pass—heedless of the simple beauty in the wayside grass. So it is with living as we rush from day to day— missing in our haste what God has planted by the way.

The Lime

The shapely lime spreads wide her boughs, the loveliest
of lovely trees—Haunted by the drowsy murmur of the
honey-hungry bees . . .

Rising from the smooth straight trunk, the cool green
branches interlace—and make a solid dome of leaves . . .
A tree of beauty, strength and grace—with power to dis-
engage its soul, releasing scents divinely sweet—
A fragrance that outstrips the breeze in glade and
garden, lane and street.

JUNE 28TH

By the Lily Pond

From the hidden mud-clogged roots have come these
lovely things—Delicate and perfect, with exquisite
colourings . . . Marvelling, I've watched and seen the
folded buds unclose— ivory and alabaster, gold and
white and rose.

Pale upon the sunlit pool the water lilies lie—in the
shadows and the clouds of the reflected sky. And round
the green isles of the leaves the dragonflies in flight—set
the air a-quivering with streaks of rainbow light.

Happy Memories

It is always summer when I walk in Memory Lane—for
you are there to greet me. Side by side we stroll again—
along the pathways of the past. No cloud to mar the
blue—not shadow dims the sunshine when I'm walking
there with you.

For the heart remembers only happiness. No tears . . .
Only what was best and sweetest of the golden years . . .
I forget the loneliness, the partings and the pain.
It is always summer when I walk in Memory Lane.

JUNE 30TH

The Half Way Mark

Half way through the year we say goodbye to June
again—the month that brought the roses to the garden
and the lane. Though the rose still blooms and there is
new life everywhere—green corn springing in the field
and flower scents on the air—there comes a pang
because you know the best of it has gone.

There is beauty still to come. The glory will go on—but
June's end is a milestone on the roadway of the year.
And those in tune with Nature's moods can't help but
shed a tear—knowing that Time presses on with steps
unfaltering. Another year of life half gone—and summer
on the wing!

July

Always New

I thought I knew all about roses—but every time
they appear—I see as a bright bud uncloses—a beauty
unnoticed last year . . . They never repeat a perfor-
mance—No season is ever the same . . . I thought I
had seen all the colours, the crimson, the gold and the
flame—but here is a rose peeping in at the door. I swear
that I never saw this one before.

I thought I knew all about thrushes,—but must admit
I was wrong—At dusk or when morning sky flushes—
they come with a new kind of song. . . The notes they
have practised since Eden—I know them by heart theme
by theme—and yet when they sing in my garden—
I listen as if in a dream—They sing the old songs with
the same measured range—yet something about it is
wondrous and strange . . . Bored we become with
what science supplies—but Nature is always an
endless surprise.

Summer Butterfly

Happiness is something like a summer butterfly—First
it's here and then it's there, forever flitting by—never
settling anywhere, but always on the wing. It can't be
bought or caught or pinioned: an elusive thing.

So when God sends happiness don't question how
or why. Take it where you find it. Thankful be, and
never try—to understand from whence it comes.
Enjoy the present hour. Happiness is rare and is as
fleeting as a flower.

Seek it and you miss it, but it seems to come your
way—when you least expect it. You awake one lovely
day—to find a new song in your heart, a new light in
the sky. Seize the golden moment. It is only passing by.

Holidays Abroad

She takes her holidays abroad. She couldn't possibly
think of Frinton or St. Leonards, Keswick or Torquay. . .
One has to get away, she says, from prunes and apple
pie. From porridge, beef and batter pudding, (but I can't
think why).

The English weather gets her down. It really is too
much. She adores the sun, you know: the continental
touch! The Costa Brava, Paris, Rome, Biarritz or some
such place. But she packs a mac and takes a woolly—
just in case.

She scribbles postcards to her friends from places
strange and grand. Having fun in Austria, in France or
Switzerland . . . but sometimes (tell it not in Gath) she
wonders wistfully—about that place near Bognor where
they give you shrimps for tea!

Passing By

If only we could check the speed of time—and make the season stop at summer's prime! If only we could bid the roses stay as lovely as we see them now today!

But if we could perform this miracle—would their beauty seem so wonderful? Would it look so fair or mean so much—an everlasting rose death could not touch? . . . Summers lovelier seem as on they fly—because we know how quickly life slips by.

JULY 5TH

One Perfect Day

Did you ever live one perfect day—When everything you did or said or thought—was in the spirit of the One who brought—the light of life to guide us on our way? Did you ever feel when night brought rest—and your heavy lids began to close—that in every matter that arose—you had practised what you had professed?

No. You never did, for are not we—fallible and human? None is good. We know so much, yet have not understood—the simple truth Christ preached in Galilee . . . We fail, as all must fail unless they pray—for strength of will to keep the soul alive. Tomorrow, while there's time, resolve to strive—to conquer self—and live one perfect day.

Leaf Language

What are the green leaves whispering? What do the tall trees say?—down in the deep woods talking, all through the night and day. Huddled together secretly—murmuring in the rain . . . Is it of grief or rapture? Is it of joy or pain?

Tender and soft and beautiful—Voices from fairyland . . . speaking a mystic language—no man can understand.

This Is England

Foxgloves ring their dappled bells along the leafy lanes—Honeysuckle twines about the cottage window panes . . . Woods are fringed with willow-herb, and scarlet poppies blow—in the rippling cornfields as the breezes come and go.

On trellised porch and weathered wall the rambling rose unfolds. Every little garden path is gay with marigolds. The country airs are burdened with the warm sweet scent of hay. This is England . . . This is England on a summer's day.

Passing Seasons

From the meadows now there comes the fragrant scent
of new mown hay. Men are busy in the fields from
break of dawn till close of day.

The shining blade has done its work upon the gently
waving grass. The first crop cut, the year half gone . . .
How quickly now the days will pass!

Yet, all seasons bring their blessings. Why lament the
changing scene? . . . In one field the hay is stacked—and
in the next—the corn is green.

As Roses Have Thorns

As roses have thorns, so does love have its times
  of testings, frustrations and pains.
But what is it worth if it cannot withstand
  the pressure, the heartaches and strains?

Love's depths can't be measured by kiss, word or gift—
  but by sympathy tender and true;
the will to forbear, to forgive,
to forget, and to take the most generous view—
hiding the scars and the stings that still smart,
ready to laugh and to make a new start.

The Glory of a Garden

Read not through the dusty tomes that hold the
world's philosophy—if for God your soul is seeking—
In your garden you will see—proof beyond the heart's
desiring—of the Mind behind all things: scent and
colour of the flowers; the hum of bees; the beat
of wings.

Greater proof could not be given of the wonder of
His ways—than the glory of a garden—in the golden
summer days.

Reminders

Cast your eye across the country looking north, south,
east or west—and the symbol of our faith in flint or
brick or stone expressed—you will see on towers and
steeples pointing to the sky above—the uplifted cross
of Christ, a silent witness to the Love—that enfolds the
towns and hamlets where the parish churches stand—
Mute reminders of the God who holds the whole world
in His hands.

Lovely Day

O Lovely day when everything—conspires to make a
sad heart sing. O lovely day of sun-bright skies—of fiery
flowers with golden eyes—and fruit aflush upon the
spray. O lovely day! O lovely day!

A day that promises so much. Awake me with a magic
touch and bring me back to life again. After drought,
the healing rain.

I see the rose beside the door—as something never seen
before. The blackbird singing in the tree—is singing, so
it seems, for me . . . The long dark night has passed
away. O lovely day! O lovely day!

Leaving School

Schooldays will be over when the term comes to an
end—I hate to think that we shall have to say goodbye,
my friend—but always I'll remember in the years that
are to be—the good and happy friendship that has
meant so much to me.

Many a life-long friendship has begun at school and so—let
us vow to keep in touch wherever we may go . . . Whatever
Time may hold in store these memories will remain. Good
luck to you, my dearest friend—until we meet again.

Blue Silk

Like a scarf of bright blue silk the narrow English Channel lies—Soft and smooth, without a ripple, shining under cloudless skies . . . Blue silk fringed with frills of lace where white-edged waves break lazily. Can this be our bastion, this silky smiling summer sea?

This strip of water that today appears so calm and beautiful—is the bulwark of an Empire, mighty and impregnable . . . The wall of steel, the iron ramparts that throughout the centuries—have been our first line of defence, and saved us from our enemies.

JULY 15TH

The Flying Sunbeam

Like a flying sunbeam it flits about the flowers up and down the colonnades amongst the lupin towers—in and out the lavender that lines the border beds. With an airy fairy grace alighting on the heads of the sunflowers, bold as brass, that stare above the hedge, resting with its wings a-quiver on a petal's edge. Clinging like a feather to the red dome of the phlox, swinging round the rosy steeples of the hollyhocks. A streak of gold upon the wind, a brightness flashing by. One of God's small miracles: a yellow butterfly.

The Truth Comes Home

There is always something that your heart is longing for—something to complete your happiness. You are always wanting something else and something more—just one other thing you would possess.

But when you get that precious pearl it proves to be a stone—until at last the truth comes home to you. That life is dull and meaningless if lived for self alone. It isn't what you get but what you do—that brings contentment to the heart and real friends to your door—the kind you never find while you are wanting something more.

Flower of the Sun

It came out of a packet, the seed from which it grew.
This glowing golden sunflower has grown the summer
through—and now stands tall and radiant. The bloom
triumphant towers—shining like a little sun above the
other flowers.

Yet it's nothing grand or rare—A common sight to see—
in any country garden. And it always seems to be—
unconscious of its splendour as it hangs there bright and
high—thrusting up out of the earth as if to reach the
sky.

Lovely sunflower, come to teach a lesson to the proud.
There you stand in all your glory with your head
unbowed—homely, unpretentious, yet your beauty
draws the eye—and warms the cockles of the heart of
every passer-by.

Seek Ye First

Where to find direction in the chaos all around? That's
the question. Where can peace and happiness be found?
. . . How can one pursue the high and finer things of
life—when the world is torn with hatreds, selfishness
and strife?

Seek ye first God's Kingdom. Other guests are all in
vain—bringing disappointment and frustration in their
train—if we have not sought and found the thing
beyond all price: the Truth the Master came to teach
through love and sacrifice.

Seek ye first this precious pearl—before all other things—
Nothing else will satisfy or give the spirit wings—to rise
above despair and with a faith triumphant face—the evils
and the ills that now beset the human race.

Cottage Garden

What could be more lovely on a golden summer day
than this old cottage garden somewhere Surrey way.
Lupins like bright candles burning in the sultry air.
Poppies like red wisps of paper in the sun's fierce glare.
Pansies dreaming by the borders—wide-eyed, in a
   trance.
Boughs of apple shuffling shadows where the sunbeams
   dance.
Butterflies with powdered wings and drowsy droning
   bees.
Scent of full-blown cabbage roses drifting on the breeze.
Passionflowers that fall across the lattice in a shower.
Who am I, dear God, that I should have this perfect
   hour?

JULY

Family Holidays

Be kind to the kiddies on holiday. Although there's so much to be done—Be patient and calm and good-tempered. A harsh word can spoil all the fun . . . The children get tired and excited—and quickly the tears start to flow. You're harassed and hot and exhausted—and cross too—but don't let it show! Be happy while all still together. One day when you're scattered apart—This holiday you will remember and may it bring joy to your heart—with nothing to mar recollections and nothing to hurt or upset—make it the happiest ever with never a word to regret.

JULY 21ST

The Shallows and the Deeps

Quiet and shallow are the waters where the leafy
  willows sway.
Yet this little winding river flowing gently on its way
Is going out to meet the sea and swell the ocean's
  rolling tide.
The stream will widen to embrace the mighty waves
  where great ships ride.

Uneventful life may seem, a narrow stream of nights and days
Yet somewhere in the future it will open into broader ways.
Every soul in God's own time is called unto its destiny—
To steer its course alone upon the waters of Eternity.

Tomorrow's Burden

Don't pick up Tomorrow's burden while it's still
Today. Hour by hour we're given strength our part in
life to play—Light sufficient to illume the path that
we must tread—Not enough to pierce the darkness of
the miles ahead . . .

We in some mysterious way are helped when things go
wrong—Shoulders stoop beneath the strain—and yet we
get along—finding that we have the power to meet each
fresh demand—if we reach out in the dark and hold the
unseen Hand.

Never look for storms approaching when the skies you
scan. Don't anticipate the future; it's not ours to plan.
Do not strain your eyes to see the turnings in the road.
Why take on before you must another extra load?

Don't go searching down the byways for the things you
fear. There's no need to fight the next day's battle till
you hear—the summons of the trumpet and the beating
of the drums. Don't pick up Tomorrow's burden till
Tomorrow comes.

Summer Moonlight

When summer moonlight trails a silver ribbon on the sea—I remember other summers. Things come back to me. Things I thought I had forgotten. Time strange tricks will play—something from the long ago will seem like yesterday.

When beneath a rising moon the sea lies shimmering—the magic never fails to work, for always it will bring—those enchanted summers back when life and love were new—when all the world belonged to me and every dream came true . . . That was years ago and yet how real it seems to be—when summer moonlight trails a silver ribbon on the sea.

The Sea

The seas that break around our shores are changing all the while. Sometimes round the cliffs and coves in mounting waves they pile, grey and angry, wild and stormy, spouting jets of spray—cold and cruel and dangerous—upon a summer day.

Then the weather takes a turn, the wind drops suddenly. The mood has changed to one of calm and blue tranquillity. Wavelets ripple, breaking gently in a lacy frill. Sunlight puts a glaze of gold on waters warm and still . . . Night too works its magic when a moon above the sea, turns the gold to silver, pewter, pearl and ebony.

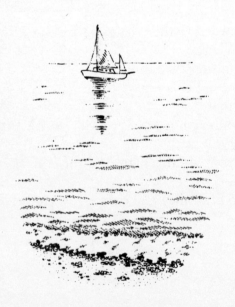

Lovers' Lane

It's lovely in the summer days—a perfect lovers' lane.
It's shady in the sunshine and it's fragrant in the rain;
the wild flowers in the hedges fling their perfume on
  the breeze.
From dawn to dusk the birds trill out their music in
  the trees . . .
When day is ended and the world is wrapped in
  evening's calm,
the lovers down the leafy lane go strolling arm in arm;
they dream Love's gay romantic dreams, exploring
  magic realms,
until the moon comes peeping through the tangle of
  the elms . . .

Then homeward to the village where the lighted
  windows gleam,
enchanted in the secret rapture of a lover's dream . . .
What ardent hopes are harboured in the heart of
  man and maid!
The common earth is holy ground when, brave and
  unafraid,
they view from youth's high peak of faith the years that
  are to be—
and heart to heart they make their vows for all Eternity . . .

Oh, may they never lose this sense of magic and delight
that clings about them as they walk, enraptured,
    through the night.
No matter what the years may hold of pleasure or of
    pain,
may life for them be one long stroll along lover's lane.

JULY 26TH

Three Days

Three Days and three days only are really your
concern—So drop the futile worries and let the seasons
turn . . . Three days! You'll find it simpler reducing
things this way—to yesterday, tomorrow and the
present day.

The first you cannot alter for yesterday has gone—and
though regrets still linger you have to carry on—praying
for forgiveness—There's nothing else to do—to banish
the remembrance of all that troubles you.

Tomorrow is a secret. The far horizon's rim—conceals
God's hidden purpose—so leave it all with Him. Today's
the day that matters. Today is yours to live—
So take it and be grateful for what it has to give.

Come Lovely Rose

Come lovely rose and set my garden glowing. Open your buds. Too soon they will be going . . . Make my small plot all bright and beautiful. This is your hour, your own gay festival.

Twine round the fence your pink and crimson sprays. Line every path with glorious blooms ablaze . . . Hang on my wall a tapestry of roses I shall remember when the summer closes.

Seaside Shop

In every little High Street in the towns around our shores—there are shops with spades and buckets hung around the doors. Picture postcards on a rack with all the local views. Beach bags, comics, shrimping nets, gay balls and canvas shoes.

In the window, boats and kites and sticks of rock you see. Souvenirs of painted shells, of brass and pottery . . . guide-books, maps and pencils, lemonade and ginger pop. Sweets and toys and ice-cream cones. You know the sort of shop.

In the path of so-called progress things change year by year. It would be a tragedy if they should disappear, the little shops we come to know so well on holiday. The seaside wouldn't be the same if they were swept away.

Things That You Can't Understand

The longer you've waited the sweeter it seems when summer's full tide flows at last—the longer you've sat at a window and watched the clouds and the rain driving past—the greater the joy when the sun floods the garden with waves of shimmering light—the more you are conscious of life and its mysteries, morning and noon-day and night. The longer you've waited in shadow and silence the sharper the pleasure it brings—to watch how the blackbird alights on a bough with a sweep of its fluttering wings . . . The longer you live and the more you discover the wonders of sky, sea and land—the more you are baffled and silenced in awe at the things that you can't understand.

A Quiet Moment Here and There

If you would advance you must retreat into the calm—
to be found within yourself: the place where there is
balm—for wounded heart and weary spirit. Only there
you find—easement for the strains and stresses of the
daily grind.

If you would go forward you must take a few steps
back—deep into the inner world to seek the thing you
lack. There in silence absolute to hold and to possess—
the precious pearl of quietude, the jewel of happiness.

Don't go rushing on non-stop. You need a break each
day—to relieve the tension, to reflect, to rest, to pray . . .
Minds and bodies cannot stand the worry and the
wear—of modern life without a quiet moment here
and there.

Always the Best

Always look your best though no-one else is there
to see. Always make the best of things wherever you
may be. Always put your best into the job you have
to do—Place the best construction of what's said or
done to you.

Always play your best though no-one's there to keep the
score. Always show your best face when there's someone at the door. The best foot forward gets you home—
you do not need to run. Always see the best and not the
worst in everyone.

August

Passing on the Blessing

Holidays are in the air. There's talk of going here and there—planning cruises, tours and trips—in planes and trains and cars and ships . . . But don't forget that even in these days of affluence—there are many who will never ever get a chance—to have a change from the routine and go off to the sea. On incomes fixed and small they can't afford such luxury.

So if you're a lucky one with happy days in view— demonstrate your gratitude; give up an hour or two— and give to someone not so blessed an outing or a treat—something to look forward to; such things can make life sweet . . . To those who never have the pleasure of a holiday—pass a blessing on for every good that comes your way.

The Wind in the Wheatfield

The wheat is like a sun-flecked sea beneath the summer sky—little ripples break the surface as the wind slips by . . . Here and there the scarlet poppies with their petals wide—rise and dip like red-sailed vessels on the rolling tide.

Crisp and dry the wheatears rustle as the tall stalks sway—the sound that is the sweetest sound of this most perfect day: the sighing and the whispering of newly ripened grain—-the roving of the restless wind across the golden plain.

Try to Remember

When you're cooped up inside on a beautiful day and you long to be out in the sun—walking or working at something or other and having your own kind of fun— you feel you're hard-done-by, self pity creeps in, you resent being tied and on call—but try to remember the sick and afflicted and those who can't get out at all.

The clock will soon strike and will give you your freedom to fling off the harness you wear—but they will remain where they are night and day with no hope of a breath of fresh air . . . So try not to grumble when outside it's fine with a bright sunny sky overhead—many would like to be there in your shoes, instead of just lying in bed.

The Holidays

Train the children not to waste the precious holiday hours—Teach them how to think and look at berries, leaves and flowers—Educate the little ones to study Nature's ways—Open a new and wonderful world for them in holidays.

Freed from schoolroom let them wander, wondering at it all—Let them see the glorious splendour of a waterfall—Draw their active minds away from mere mechanical toys—discovering the magic of strange things and deeper joys.

Of richly-painted butterflies and graceful birds in flight—of sun and shadow breaking through the curtain of the light—Woods where great trees lean above a softly singing brook—Feed them with the knowledge to be found in Nature's book.

Rose in the Rain

Rose at the window pressed close to the pane—lifting your face to the tears of the rain—over the hill, reaching up from the spray—Joy you have brought to an invalid's day.

Seen through the sheen of the silvery shower, keeping me company hour after hour—bright in lightning that splinters the sky—poised on your stem with the wind blowing by.

Rose at the window—I've watched from my bed—and lovely you looked with the storm overhead—What is the magic? The secret explain—How to hold on till the sun comes again.

Dreamer

Dreaming of the things you mean to do some other day.
Always dreaming of tomorrow, wishing Time away.
Dreaming of the happiness that is eluding you.
Never doing anything to make the dream come true.

Dreaming of the lovely things you think you want or need.
Dreaming of the roses, never working at the weed.
Dreaming of a goal but never shouldering a load—
And really setting out to face the hazards of the road.

Dreaming of a harvest when you never touch a plough.
Dreaming of the future and forgetting Life is NOW.

AUGUST 7TH

Out into the Sunshine

I'm looking in a new direction, encompassing a wider
view. I'm trusting in the One who loves me—and knows
me through and through.

I'm opening the gates of freedom—escaping from my
small dark cell. I'm walking out into the sunshine—
knowing all is well.

The Weavers

Overnight the weavers spin a web of silver strands: a web as fine as gossamer, untouched by human hands. . . From twig to twig and stem to stem the fairy mesh is spread; a perfect pattern, dew-embroidered, worked in silken thread.

The golden arrows of the sun strike down on flower and tree—A sudden wind shakes leaf and bough—and presently we see—ragged shreds of tattered lacework, torn beyond repair. But tomorrow morning there'll be new webs everywhere.

AUGUST 9TH

Doing Something Different

The value of a holiday cannot be assessed—by the number of miles you travel north, south, east or west. You may plan a holiday and dream up something grand—covering great distances by air or sea or land, but there is no magic in the act of travelling—a journey that takes you away from home may or may not bring—the sort of rest you really need. The good of holidays—lies in change and in departure from the well worn ways—Doing something different, the set routine to shatter. Five miles off or hundreds . . . well, it doesn't really matter.

Riverside Reverie

Watching how the swallows skim with swiftness and
with grace—where the branches of the weeping willows
interlace . . . Noting how the rushes quiver in the
restless breeze—how the rays of golden light are sifted
through the trees.

Lulled into contentment by the water flowing by—
underneath the lovely ceiling of the quiet sky . . .
Resting by the river-side—life's problems pass away—
and fade like mists into the peace and beauty of the day.

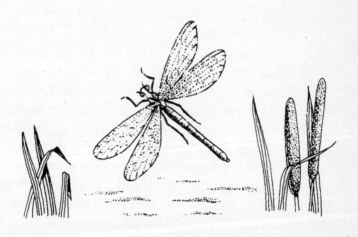

Summer Storm

An hour ago the garden lay all drowsy, still and warm—
but now there's chaos and confusion, madness, stress
and storm. The lilies writhe, tormented by the slashing
of the rain, the roses lose their grip as on the trellises
they strain.

The hollyhocks that yesterday stood brave and bright
and tall, are humbled, bent and broken as they sway
against the wall. The lovely blue delphiniums collapse
like leaning towers—battered to the ground amongst the
bruised and weeping flowers.

As suddenly come storms into life. Out of the summer
calm—there springs a wind of change that's full of men-
ace and alarm. And then we know how good they were,
those days by Heaven sent, when nothing stirred the
quiet mind or marred the heart's content.

Does It Matter?

When all is said and done—Does it matter—if you're in
the third or seventh place? If neighbours have some
gadgets that you covet—or colleagues streak ahead in
life's made race? No, if you have friends who really love
you—and strength to bear the cross upon the back—So
long as you can rest with conscience easy—at peace
with God and man—What can you lack?

When all is said and done—Does it matter—the thing
you won't forget and won't forgive . . . ? A grievance
nursed can grow beyond controlling. Stop worrying.
Step out of it and live.

Mountain Pastures

A track runs through the heather like a ribbon thin and
white—Round the steeply rising ledge and up the
fir-clad height . . . Through the clouds in mist and
shadow winds the narrow trail—leading to the
mountain pastures high above the vale.

For centuries unnumbered men have brought their
flocks to graze—on the grassy slopes that lie along
these lovely ways. . . And still to-day in pastures
green beside the falling rills—the shepherd comes to
feed his sheep upon the quiet hills.

Wonderful Day

If you're looking for things to be awkward about then
  you won't have to look very far.
A hundred excuses for making complaints you can find
  on the spot where you are.
Life hands you a grievance as soon as you rise, if your
  thoughts take that natural line.
There'll always be something to start you off grumbling
  if you are determined to whine.

Don't let it happen. As soon as you wake, get your
  mind in the right sort of frame.
Whatever comes up take it well, take it gaily. It's all in
  the luck of the game.
Look for the best and the good things in life and you'll
  find in a strange sort of way,
They come to the one who can greet every morning
  expecting a wonderful day.

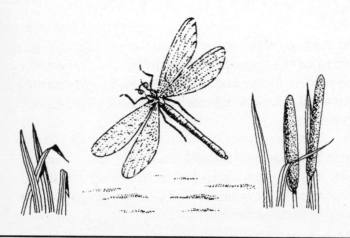

The New Forest

Here grew the oaks, the mighty oaks, from whose stout hearts our fathers made—the wooden walls of Nelson's day: the little English ships that laid—the first foundations of our strength upon the waters of the sea; the glory of our naval power; the greatness of our history.

Here grew the yews, the noble yews, from which the archer's bow was made—Here in this Hampshire wilderness of rambling wood and cloistered glade . . . Here where the immemorial trees about our paths shadows cast—the wind blows through the boughs and brings a haunting echo from the past.

AUGUST 16TH

The Harvest Scene

Old as man, yet ever lovely, pleasing to the eye: the pattern of the harvest fields beneath the August sky . . . The golden sheaves of gathered corn in long unbroken rows—Like a picture breathing peace, contentment and repose.

Much has gone into the making of this quiet scene: ploughing up the frosted earth on mornings bleak and keen . . . Money and machinery and human diligence—The sunshine and the rainfall and the Lord's good providence.

One Day's Journey

Go your way with one day's load—but not along tomorrow's road. You are not asked to walk that track—until it's on the almanac. Until today has faded out—you do not need to think about—what tomorrow's going to bring. A good thought, that, to which to cling.

Do not face until you must—tomorrow's problems— Let the dust—of one day's troubles settle first. Don't anticipate the worst. When the going's rough and tough—One day's journey is enough.

Heather Time

Now upon the hills and heaths and in the glens and glades—the heather blooms, and deepens into softly glowing shades—of lavender and amethyst: a carpet richly laid—in tones of blue and mauve and purple, wonderfully made.

Heather time in Britain! Scenes of beauty and delight— rolling plains of Hampshire—Devon moor and Scottish height . . . Many an exile dreams of this—away across the sea—walking in the heather on the hills of memory.

Going Away and Coming Home

Going away is so exciting, packing up your things—setting out by ship or road or rail, taking wings and flying off into the clouds to places strange or new. Or perhaps the known and the familiar pleases you—and so you go back once again to tread remembered ways—a well loved spot where you have spent so many holidays.

Coming home is thrilling too. It all seems kind of strange—You've had your break from the routine, you've had your needed change—but now it's over and although there's work to start once more—It's nice to walk across the threshold of your own front door. And when the garden you inspect, there'll be a weed or two—but what a joy to see the flowers you planted welcome you!

A Friend

A friend is someone who will always try to understand,
  one in whom you can confide when things get out
  of hand . . .
Someone who will listen when by bad luck you've been hit,
 never offering advice unless you ask for it.

So grapple him, said Shakespeare to your heart with
  hoops of steel.
Lonely you will never be and hopeless never feel,
if you have a friend like this when crosses you must
  bear.
You may not meet for months, but when he's needed
  . . . he'll be there.

The Fountain

In the long-neglected garden stood the fountain dry and bare. No lovely jet of sparkling water rose into the summer air, to splash into the lily pools where dragon-flies lay quivering. Without the water the fountain died; a lump of stone, a cold dead thing.

In a long-neglected house a life was lived walled in by grief. A grudge was harboured in the heart, a grievance nursed without relief. The springs of happiness were choked and love denied in all its ways. How sad when a soul dries up and dies like a fountain where no water plays!

AUGUST 22ND

The Soil Provides...

Britain's soil is bountiful—it flings its riches wide—
Scattering across the land the gold of harvest-tide . . .
The fields are bright and beautiful with grain and crops and hay—The orchards flush with swelling fruit, the gardens fair and gay.

Britain's soil is generous. No barren place is seen. Heather grows upon the heath—and meadows deep and green, offer rich sweet grasses where the flocks and herds can feed . . . The earth is good. The soil provides, and meets our every need.

Weeds

When you're weeding in the garden, heartless you must be—It's fatal to examine what you root out ruthlessly: golden-headed dandelions and sorrel's crimson plumes. Nettles, bindweed, buttercups will put out dainty blooms if left to flower in Nature's way, and every time you mow—you destroy how many daisies! White and gold they grow—marring with their tiny heads the lawn so neatly green. If you want to have the finest garden ever seen—blind your eyes to the perfection of intruding life: clover, groundsel, pimpernel. Continue in the strife—against these wild unwanted things and stop them bearing seeds—unceasing in the war upon the wild flowers we call weeds.

The Afterglow

Loveliest of memories! Stay on inside my heart—whatever else may fade away as passing years depart—Linger like the fragrance of a rose at summer's height—never failing to evoke perpetual delight.

Loveliest of memories! that glorious golden day—that perfect day of happiness with sunshine all the way—when everything was wonderful—when life and love were new—and just like a fairytale a lovely dream come true.

Time may dim the colours. Things must change as days go on—but when the glow has faded and the first gay rapture gone—The afterglow of happiness together we'll recall: the loveliest of memories: the loveliest of all.

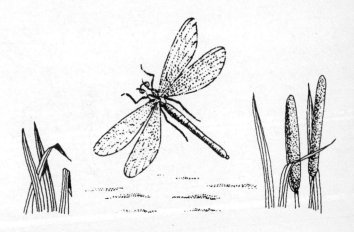

Never Rest Content

Be contented with your life, but not with how you live.
Never rest content with what you do and what you
give. Always go on trying to improve on yesterday—
brightening the path for someone else along the way.

Be happy and be satisfied with what you now possess—
but never with yourself. Be ever ready to confess—your
faults and failings. Grumble less and do a little more—
to make yourself a nicer person than you were before.

Do not be too sure that all is right and well with you.
Keep on checking up on all you think and say and do.
Be contented even though you've found no lucky star. Be
content with what you have, but not with what you are.

Herbaceous Border

In the border by the wall are flowers of every hue—
Marigolds along the edge and cornflowers pink and blue . . .
Phlox and gay chrysanthemum and vivid dahlia.
Sunflowers in a glowing mass and haze of lavender.

And burning brightly through the glory of these August
days—the pokers lift their brilliant blooms like torches all
ablaze—Flaming at the Gates of Autumn as the first leaves
fall—Lighting up the last glad days of Summer's carnival.

AUGUST 27TH

Be still and Listen

How can He come to an unquiet mind? How show
His face to the inwardly blind? How can a sense of
His presence be caught—in the confusion of turbulent
thought?

If you would savour the calm of that peace—stop, wait
and listen. Let questionings cease. Sit in the silence. Be
still and believe—that you at His hands a great gift will
receive—of healing and blessing . . . Doubt not He will
come—as once to the lame and the deaf and the
dumb—He came with new life—to revive and restore.
Make ready your heart for He stands at the door.

Give Your Love

Give your love to others. Don't spend it on yourself.
Give your heart's good treasure. Don't hoard it on the
shelf . . . Give a word of comfort. Give a helping hand.
Give where it is needed. Try to understand.

Give the best that's in you to the job you do. Give the
world your blessing and it blesses you . . . Give your life
to something that is well worth while. Give—and never
ever forget to give a smile.

Time Leaps On

Every summer goes more swiftly than the one before.
Time moves faster. Weeks go quicker. Though you may
ignore—the dates upon the calendar, pretending it's not
so—the summer sunshine fades too soon into the
autumn glow.

In childhood's bright and timeless seasons summer
lingers long—the blackbirds and the thrushes sing a
never-ending song—and there are always roses. But alas
as old we grow—the pace of Life is quickened. Time
leaps on. The hours once slow—seem to fly away from
us on wings that go too fast and every summer passing
by is shorter than the last.

The Apple Tree

It's never pruned or sprayed, but left to Nature's tender care—No one knows how many years it has been standing there—casting dappled shadows on the little cottage plot—lifting high its leafy arms above the chimney pot. A living thing, a lovely thing, this old, old, apple tree. About its boughs the children play and birds make melody . . . And every year bowed down with fruit the heavy branches bend—crowned with gold and crimson glory at the Summer's end.

The Fragrance of Goodwill

It's the warming of the sun that draws the fragrance up— from new-mown grass and freshly furrowed clay . . . it's the warmth that lures the scent out of the flowery cup— that opens to the glory of the day.

It's the warmth of loving thoughts that melts the icicle— in hearts where grief has left a bitter chill . . . it's the warming touch of love that works the miracle—and conjures forth the fragrance of goodwill.

September

The Magic of September

What is it that lends a magic to September days?
The sparkly mornings bright with dew, the pearly
evening haze? The glow of fruit on laden boughs,
plum, damson, apple and pear? The sense of peace
and of fulfilment brooding everywhere?

"The resurrection of the roses opening again—blooming
for a second time as summer starts to wane?" . . . The
creepers turning red and gold, a strange and glorious
sight. The swallows grouping for the making of their
southward flight. The sunflowers and the dahlias and
chrysanthemums ablaze . . . what is the secret of the
magic of September days?

Beyond the Silence

The garden seems a quiet place but listen and you'll hear—sounds beyond the silence that escape the untrained ear: the hum of flies, the sleepy mumbling of the bumble bees—the rustling of the wind between the branches of the trees.

An apple falling to the ground, the fluttering of wings. The voices of the singing birds, the stir of hidden things. The whisper of the raindrops as they touch the sun-baked ground. The garden wrapped in outward peace is full of life and sound.

Reliability

When you make a promise, keep it, trifling though it be.
Win a reputation for reliability.
Never go back on your word or disappoint your friends.
Don't do something mean and weak, then rush to make
  amends.

Can you be relied upon to carry through a plan?
Can you be relied upon to do the best you can?
Are you to be trusted in some great emergency?
Can you take the weight of a responsibility?

Fickle folks draw fickle friends, and many friends mean
  none.
In this world we're truly lucky if we find but one.
One faithful friend that needs no vow, no gift, no bribe,
  no tie.
One true and dear and trusted friend on whom we may
  rely. . .

And such a friend comes not by chance. Life's laws are
  good and just,
for friendship such as this is built on honour, faith and
  trust.

Prelude

In the orchards ripe fruit falling from the heavy trees—
Shaken from the loaded boughs with every passing
 breeze.
Blackberries in ripening clusters in the country lanes.
Chill of twilight—hint of winter—as the daylight wanes.
Tint of crimson in the leaves where trailing creepers
 climb.
Sheaves of corn out in the fields . . . the crown of
 Summertime.
Prelude of the Autumn . . . Morning mist and evening
dew.
The haze that rests like purple smoke upon the distant
 view.
Soon the sunshine will be fading and the birds take
 wing.
Till the world rolls round again towards another Spring.

Sunlight and Heather

Purple and gold was the moor that day. The world lay behind us, far away—And swiftly the shining hours went by—Under the wide, warm Devon sky.

That was indeed pure happiness. The last we should know. How could we guess? Already the shadow of Fate was there—stealing upon us unaware.

Sunlight and heather! That's all I see—Set in the frame of memory. . . Strange that this scene should linger on—long after you yourself have gone.

The Apple-harvest

Ripe and red the apples hang upon the thickly fruited spray—Glowing in the mellow sunlight of the golden autumn day. . . Up and down the dappled aisles, all day the busy pickers pass—and children with their little baskets search for windfalls in the grass.

Ladders resting on the branches; wagons waiting in the lane. The age-old scenes of apple-harvest are enacted once again. . . .Common as a field of hay—and yet it is a wondrous thing: the crimson harvest that is gathered from the blossoms of the Spring.

Once Again

Once again the harvest: Rye, barley, oats and wheat. The everlasting miracle. The cycle is complete. . . the seed in spring or autumn sown has ripened into grain. Gold and brown the corn is glowing. Harvest time again.

There's a quiet holiness about a field that stands—ready for reaping by machine or human hands. . .reverence the earth as part of God's eternal plan. Feed it, love it—save it from rapacity of man.

September 8th

New Girl

The road you start today runs out as far as dreams can range: the road of opportunity. . . it all seems rather strange: new school, new term, new work, new hopes. A new life lies ahead—so say a prayer for guidance on the path that you must tread.

You will need it. There'll be much to turn your steps astray. Difficulties you are bound to meet all along the way. But keep your standards high, give your best and never less—then you'll surely reap in time the harvest of success. But there's something greater than the winning of a goal: the making of a character, the training of a soul. Whatever else you may achieve, whatever else you do, learn to value what is good and beautiful and true.

On the Bridge

Lovely is this old grey bridge that takes the burden of the road—Rhythmic arches gently flowing, bear with grace their daily load. . .Anglers in the deep recesses, rod in hand, stand patiently—Silent figures in a scene of undisturbed tranquility.

Time has touched with mellowed beauty every stone of span and pier. Ploughman, pedlar, lord and lady, Roundhead, King and Cavalier—All have crossed this ancient bridge upon the road to history—and stood where now I watch the river flowing down to meet the sea.

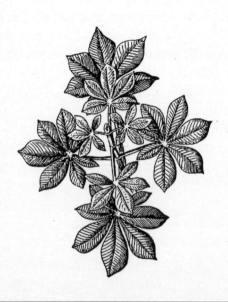

Take What Comes

Don't expect perfection for you'll never find it here.
This is earth, not heaven, so with charity and cheer
take what comes—the good, the bad, and don't start
  whimpering
when you're disappointed with a person or a thing.

Do not worship idols and complain when you have
  found
feet of clay beneath the robes in which you've wrapped
  them round . . .

Everyone is human. Do not be too critical
when someone fails, Remember that you too are fallible.

Keep your ideals in your heart and set your standard
  high,
but don't lose faith when things go wrong. Just let the
  storm blow by. . .
Do not ask too much of life or reach beyond your
  range.
Accept and learn to live content with what you cannot
  change.

Best of All

I love the April daffodils, the irises of May. I love June's gift of roses and the smell of new-mown hay. I love the solemn beauty of the lilies of July—And the blue delphiniums that match the summer sky.

. . . I love to see the rose-pink spires of August holly-hocks—high above the dahlias, the asters and the phlox; but best of all I love September with its mellow days: The month that brings the ripened berries and the fruited sprays. Chrysanthemums—and creepers turning red upon the wall. The climax of the gardener's year; to me the best of all.

A September Morning

Sunlight breaking through the mist; the birches turning gold. . . Crimson dahlias tall and lovely; Sunflowers bright and bold.

Silver webs upon the grass; a sense of peace profound. . . In the orchard fruited branches bending to the ground.

Thoughts at Harvest-time

How bored we grow with things that human beings
have designed. The scientists perform their tricks, but
do not stir the mind. Yet we never lose the thrill of
nature's wonder-screen. The never failing magic of an
ever changing scene.

Many times we've watched the cornfields turn from
green to gold. The pattern is familiar as the picture is
unrolled—but every time it happens it is strange and
fresh and new—Never does the eye grow weary of the
harvest view.

God's creations never bore. So wonderful they are! The
seed, the corn, the reaping. Morning light and evening
star. . . How dull our own inventions seem, how feeble
and how small—beside the marvellous design that lies
behind it all.

The Cycle of the Year

The last dry sheaves are gathered in. The fields of stubble lie—spread like a patchwork in the vale. And as the days go by—the pattern changes; golden acres turn to deepest brown—As the plough goes slowly over field and hill and down.

As we watch the closing scenes of summer's harvest-tide—Hour by hour the moving plough transforms the countryside. . . Ploughman, sower, reaper, gleaner—All have laboured here—in their season, to complete the cycle of the year.

Michaelmas Daisies

There they stand in spreading clumps along the border bed—in shades that range from amethyst to violet and red. Pale as lilac-tinted mist and purple royal and rich. In many new varieties. I can't tell which is which—but this I know that when I see these flowers of Michaelmas— fading leaves will soon be falling on the frosted grass.

Every season has its emblems, every phase its sign; the budding bough, the sheaf of corn, the berry and the bine— leave their own familiar mark on Nature's calendar—and so when come the daisies mauve and pink and lavender— no longer can I fool myself. It's useless to pretend. I know that autumn's really here and summer at an end.

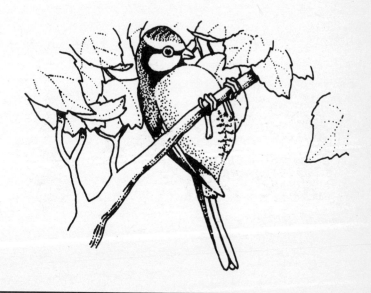

211

The Gleanings

As we glean amongst the stubbles of our memories—we recall old griefs, old heartaches and old tragedies—but why dwell on a recollection that revives past pain? Glean in happier fields and you will find much golden grain.

The loveliest things in life can still be gathered quietly there. Time the reaper has not left the future bleak and bare. . . Much remains to compensate for all the trials and tears: hope, contentment, faith and peace: the gleanings of the years.

SEPTEMBER 17TH

The Day Before

On the day before we have our Harvest Festival—we come with loaded baskets for the yearly ritual—of decorating font and pulpit, altar, ledge and sill. Each to her appointed task, we set to with a will.

At first it looks impossible to try and sort things out: carrots, marrows, apples, grapes and plums are strewn about. Flower-filled buckets line the porch amongst the sheaves of wheat, but how moving is the moment when it is complete. . . To see our loved and lovely church all bright and beautiful—garlanded in glory for tomorrow's festival.

Lose Yourself

Lose yourself with all your wants, your worry and your
    woe.
Lose yourself in other people's troubles. Yours will go . . .
Lose yourself by getting lost in someone else's maze—
helping one another through the dark unhappy days.

Lose yourself in something bigger than your own
    affairs.
Lose yourself, immersed in all the probems and the
    cares
that surround you day by day. You'll soon forget your
    own—
for you'll come to realise that you are not alone,
suffering in isolation; others suffer too.
Lose yourself to find yourself and when at last you do,
you will find a better person than you were before,
when you lived for self alone behind your own front
    door.

Redbreast

Is he singing to the swallows, bidding them good-bye—
before they take their journey south across the trackless
sky? . . . Perched upon the garden fence, he chirrups
all day long. What, I wonder, is the meaning of his
little song?

Does he sing because he likes these golden autumn
days? No, it's not a rhapsody of love or joy or praise—
He's simply claiming for his own the corner he has
found; the spot that he has chosen for his winter
feeding ground.

Telling all the other robins to "Keep Off the Grass".
Here between the cosy hedges he intends to pass—the
season of the long dark days until the Springtime
comes—Hovering around the window . . . waiting
for the crumbs.

So Lovely Is September

So lovely is September with ripeness and with bloom, we fail to see that it conceals the threat of summer's doom. So bright the garden glory, so gay the blazing beds, so beautiful the creepers—rose, purples, golds and reds—that we with eyes bedazzled by richness everywhere—scarcely hear the whisper of autumn on the air. So lovely is September, so bright the path we tread, that summer fades unheeded and dies with tears unshed.

SEPTEMBER 21ST

Have You Tried?

Discontented with your life? But there's another side. Change it. Rearrange it. Have you ever really tried?. . .

Moaning, groaning, grumbling will not get you very far. In yourself you have the power to reach up for a star. . . You can make or break your life. The choice is up to you. Rise above your circumstances. Take a different view.

Autumn

The first faint hint of what is yet to be—a pinkish tint
upon the cherry tree—The old Virginia creepers turning
red around the timbers of the garden shed—Lovely in its
dying, yet how beautiful—September's golden leaves:
the autumn miracle.

As sure as clocks and calendars—the year when growing
old—cloaks the woods in glory—bronze, crimson,
amber, gold—The fires of Nature's making, the flames
no man can stay: the mighty conflagration that runs
from day to day—Like torches blaze the branches in
wood and garden bower—September fades but not
before it lives its finest hour.

Time Steps Out

Time is slow when we are young, but as the years
proceed—Time steps out and seems to move at twice its
former speed . . . Swiftly are the milestones passed—we
see them flashing by—Quickly do the birthdays come—
Time races . . . seasons fly.

Do not bank upon the future—its not yours to plan—No
one but your Maker knows the measure of your span . . .
We should always live each day as if it were the last—the
only chance to make amends for failings of the past.

Let Hope Go Ahead

Let Hope go ahead and you follow. Let Hope go before you today. Things will be better tomorrow if Hope be in view all the way—for Hope bears no load on her shoulders—Smoothing the rocks and the ruts—she forces a path through the boulders, dismissing the ifs and the buts.

You won't be afraid to keep going—where Hope sheds a gleam on the track—for Hope with her lamp brightly glowing—moves forward and never turns back . . . she never needs goading or prodding—unflagging she makes for the height—while you in her footprints come plodding—eyes fixed on her beautiful light.

Alone you would soon give up trying. Alone you would never succeed—but Hope undismayed and undying—strides forward to give you a lead . . . And now that a new year is dawning—and unknown the road you must tread—There's nothing to fear if each morning—you're willing to send Hope ahead.

Spring Was Yesterday

It was only yesterday that I looked out to see—blackbirds nesting in the hedge and blossom on the tree—daffodils and hyacinths—and now the creepers glow—rose and crimson on the wall. Where did the Summer go?

In a flash it came and went. I tried to hold it back—by counting every moment, but it passed and in its track—Autumn weaves a leafy carpet, russet, flame and red—where the golden goblets of the crocuses were spread.

Why does time increase its pace? It should be otherwise. Every year should be longer but each one swifter flies . . . Summers used to linger, now they hurry on their way. Looking back it seems to me that Spring was yesterday.

SEPTEMBER 26TH

Utility

Every berry in the hedge—and every grain of corn—Every little blade of grass—and every seed that's borne—is a proof that there's a Mind at work in Nature's plan—conscious of the daily needs of bird and beast and man.

Everything required is there, concealed in earth or sea. But God's provisions go beyond mere dull utility—He gives us things that serve no purpose but to beautify: flowers to scent the air with fragrance—and delight the eye.

Whatever Be Your Special Need

Whatever be your special need today. Whatever be the thing you're dreading—Pray. For there is One who understands and cares. But how can God be reached except by prayers?

Unless the door of faith be opened wide, how can God come? How can He get inside—to work the miracle of Love for you—changing your world and making all things new?

Whatever be the trouble, God can bring a happy issue out of everything—but cannot intervene or have His way with the heart that knows not how to pray.

This Thing Will Pass

The wind is beating at the pane—in frantic gusts of sleeting rain—Like the lashes of a whip it falls on the windows and the walls, thrashing through the tortured trees—at the house, while I at ease—sit in comfort safe and warm—from the fury of the storm.

The demon wind must spend its force—have its hour and take its course . . . Remember this when trials increase. Rest in faith and be at peace. Through the turmoil and the din—Hear that still, small voice within—speak above the crashing brass—saying, "Trust. This thing will pass".

From a Window

The people who sit at a window and watch
as the crowds in the street pass along
see more than the people who rush to and fro
taking part in the big, noisy throng.
They get the best view of the things that occur
from the quiet of their hidden retreat,
while the folks who go pushing and jostling along
only see their small bit of the street . . .

It's the same in the swirl and chaos of life
when your world seems all frenzy and din—
just withdraw, and go into your own secret self;
looking out from the window within,
you will find that your troubles diminish and fade,
as remote as the far stars on high,
then serene in the stillness, your heart will grow wise
as you watch the mad world rushing by.

Learning to Live

It's a hard and a difficult business, this business of
　　learning to live,
Knowing how best to make use of the knowledge that
　　the passing years give.
To muster the technique of living is something not
　　learnt in a day,
For only experience teaches and time alone shows us
　　the way.

It's an art to be studied and practised, to achieve a
　　degree of success.
It's a ding-dong of trial and error: some succeed—others
　　never progress.
It takes time to discover the right way of coping with
　　people and things,
And it's not until life is half over that we learn how to
　　take what it brings.

October

We Do Not Leap from Summer

We do not leap from summer into winter's cruel grip—
scarcely noticing the changes, day by day we slip—into
autumn's gentle mood and quietly we are led—through
the lanes where turning leaves glow russet, gold and red.

Kindly is the English climate. Lovely are the links—
between the changing seasons . . . as the year in passing
sinks—into the engulfing fogs, cold winds and
frosty glaze—we walk enchanted through the magic
of October days.

OCTOBER 2ND

Stay-at-home

When the swifts and the martins have sung their good-
byes—and the swallows departed for tropical skies—He
is all the more welcome, my faithful old friend—when I
hear his sweet song at the day's quiet end.

In the massed choirs of summer he's only a note—a
melody piped from a single small throat . . . It is only
when listening in autumn's first hush—that I catch the
full song of the stay-at-home thrush.

You Go on Pretending

You go on pretending it's not really there—that tingly Octobery tang in the air. That smell of the bonfire that comes on the breeze—the flame and the gold on the shrubs and the trees . . . You try not to notice the rose-petals strewn—over the grave of the glories of June—refusing to mark how the creeper has thinned—under the comb of the blustery wind.

You go on deceiving your own foolish heart—though dahlias blacken and wither apart—touched by the frost at the morning's sharp edge—you try not to notice those gaps in the hedge . . . You hug your illusions though days are still bright—but you know—yes you know that the calendar's right. The Summer you longed for has come to an end—and now it is Autumn. What use to pretend?

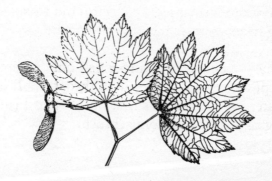

Hoping Somebody Would Call

Don't let anyone be lonely in your village or your town.
Time erects its barriers, so do your best to break them
down—before too many days go by, too many months,
too many years . . . Risk a snub and make a gesture.
Use your eyes and use your ears—to find out who's in
need of friendship and a bit of company. It's the duty of
a Christian to be kind and neighbourly.

Sometimes someone dies or to a hospital is sent away.
Circumstances come to light and then too late you hear
them say—We never knew that there was someone
living near in such distress—hoping somebody would
call to ease the ache of loneliness.

OCTOBER 5TH

Music in the Mist

Drifting mist and burning colour—all along the garden
ways . . . Blue smoke rising from the chimneys through
the soft and silvery haze.

Webs upon the spangled hedges. Wisps of gauze upon
the lawn . . . Autumn roses, pink and golden—in the
grey October dawn.

By the pond, a slim birch weeping. Sighing wind and
falling leaf—and a small bird fluting sweetly, heedless of
the tree's quiet grief.

OCTOBER 6TH

First Beginnings

Lovely are the first beginnings of the autumntide—
whether you wander afoot in woods or through the
forests ride—as the birch and bracken turn to gold and
Nature holds its breath—between the days of maturity
and its seeming hour of death.

Look your last on the year now dying. Look and let it
go. Spring will bring its resurrection. Believe; it will be
so . . . Every tree will bud, and sap will flow in every
vein. Though we, like time, must go when called; the
tree will live again.

227

October 7th

Beech Leaves

A bunch of beech leaves in a vase lights up a sunless room—and seems to bring a warming glow into the wintry gloom. A sheaf of brown and burnished leaves aglow against a wall. We see the elms and apples stripped, we watch the oak leaves fall, but beech leaves cling as if reluctant to release their hold—and so the beech outlasts the glory of the autumn gold.

Pick them now before Jack Frost appears upon the scene—press them underneath the carpet, seal with glycerine, and then they'll stand the winter through when days are dull and drear—and lend a touch of beauty to the ending of the year.

October 8th

Worth Doing

Do the job well if you do it at all—whether important or something quite small. You'll have your reward when your work you survey—and proud you can feel at the end of the day—of what you've accomplished although it may be—something that no-one is likely to see. Even although you've to answer to none—you'll know in your heart that the work was well done. In nothing be careless. In all things excel. A job that's worth doing is worth doing well.

But Never One Like This

There'll be other days, my dear, but never one like this. Never shall we know again this mood, the special bliss—of seeing golden leaves against a blue October sky—watching how they quiver as the wind goes dancing by.

You and I together walking in an autumn wood. Could there ever be a day so wonderful, so good? A day to hold and to remember to the very last. A day to treasure in the heart when other dreams have passed.

There'll be better things to do and lovelier things to see—but the present moment will remain the best for me—because it has a magic that defies analysis. There'll be other days, my dear, but never one like this.

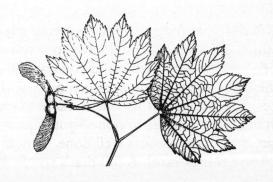

Tomorrow

Do not let your faith be shaken by the touch of sorrow,
But remember God is good and there will be tomorrow . . .
All must strive and suffer - that's the way it has to be.
Life's a skein of twisted threads: joy, laughter, tragedy.

Never doubt. Hold on and hope though hope seems all
   in vain.
Sooner than you think perhaps the sun will shine again . . .
Troubles and misfortunes come to put you to the test,
Proving strength or weakness, bringing out the worst
   and best.

No one wants to weep with you if you are always sad.
Lonely you will never be if you are brave and glad . . .
Search the clouds - you're bound to find a gleam of
   light to follow
Though today is grim and grey . . . remember there's
   tomorrow.

A Lovely Autumn Day

Autumn wraps these Islands in a cloak of foggy grey—
but here and there and now and then you get a lovely
day—when, just like the smile of God, the sun comes
breaking through—amd every corner of your world is
lighted up for you.

The dreary street is suddenly transformed before your
eyes. The garden stirs out of its sleep and wakens in
surprise—to feel on earth and grass and stone the sunshine's warm caress—and through the house there runs
a bubbling stream of happiness. Faces brighten.
Pavements turn to gold beneath your tread—for
somehow life looks different with a blue sky overhead.

Red Shawls

The little old-world cottages along the village street—
look so warm and snug beneath their thatches, thick
and neat . . . And when the autumn creepers drape the
windows and the walls—they look like dear old
grannies wrapped in bright and cosy shawls.

Their crimson cloaks grow tattered when the winds of
winter blow—the tumbling walls are left exposed to
rain and frost and snow . . . But they have stood the test
of Time—so maybe after all—it doesn't really matter
when the leaves begin to fall.

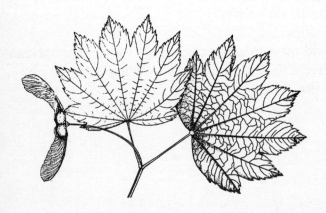

Old Age

Old Age never comes to us when Youth is in the mind.
When we have left the wild, ecstatic days of Spring
  behind
we come upon a richer time of deep content and peace,
when all the heart's red wounds are healed, and our
  rebellions cease . . .
When quiet hours bring memories that steal from out
  the years—
and lift us up on wings of dreams, and sorrow
  disappears
And only happiness remains from all the crowded past,
if we have gathered to ourselves the things that really
  last.

The body may be broken, but the mind may still expand
and touch the rosy fringes of that good and better land . . .
The spirit is forever young. Unfettered it can rise
and probe the secrets of the wind, the stars, the trees,
  the skies . . .
The old may go adventuring to seek the heart's desire
and live a thousand lives again when dreaming by
  the fire.

The Legacy

When I see October leaves glow red in wood and lane, my thoughts drift back across the months and I recall again, fragments that have lingered in the corners of the mind—the residue of beauty that the summer left behind.

There were big events for they were days of destiny. But it's not the fateful hours that haunt my memory. It is the remembered scent of lilac in the rain and honeysuckle seen by moonlight at the window pane.

That evening when the thrushes sang until the stars pricked through! That morning when it seemed that God had made the world anew . . . and that moment when I saw a cottage wall ablaze, with roses burning gold and crimson in the sun's warm haze. Pictures in the memory that nothing can destroy. Nature's lovely legacy of unforgotten joy.

The Old Dress

The beech retains the burnished beauty of her Autumn foliage—Though the dawns are sharp with frost—and through the woods the wild winds rage.

Against the gloom of pine and cypress—standing glorious and gay . . . Like a challenge to the Winter on a dark and sunless day.

The beech tree loves her faded dress—and to the old leaves she will cling—Until she's ready to put on the new green finery of Spring.

OCTOBER 16TH

Face It

Try to make a bad day brighter though the outlook's grey and drear—and a good day even better; keep the blue skies blue and clear—Make your weather. Bring the sun out. Make the effort and you'll find—You can change your circumstances if you change them in your mind.

Face the thing that now confronts you, not in a defeatist mood—but with thoughts that give you courage, faith and hope and fortitude. . . Though your fear may hover round. Outstare its grim and grisly face—Deny it. It will disappear and you'll see angels in its place—bringing good things unto you—and bits of heaven breaking through.

The Quiet Ways

Walk slowly when you walk in lanes for there is much to see—the russet bracken on the banks, the structure of a tree—when autumn winds have stripped it naked, bare against the sky. You'll never know what you have missed, if rushed, you hurry by.

Tread softly when you enter churches. This is holy ground. A mind attuned to quietness can catch the muffled sound—of all the prayers and all the praises that have risen here. Voices echo in the silence for the listening ear.

Go gently as you go along the noisy ways of life. Move graciously amongst the crowds, the turmoil and the strife . . . Speak lovingly to children, to the stranger and the friend. Speak kindly. Never with your tongue your fellow man offend.

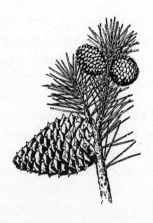

To the Cedar

Do you ever sigh with envy when you see the other trees—Gorgeous in their autumn splendour—all a-shimmer in the breeze—Decked as if for carnival with coloured ribbons, bright and bold . . . Do you ever envy them their finery of red and gold?

Stately cedar, tall and graceful in your gown of sober hue—Envy not your pretty sisters—for within a month or two—They'll be stripped of every rag—while you'll stand quiet and serene—Mantled in your winter beauty . . . Ever lovely, ever green.

October 19th

Autumn Crocuses

Underneath the weeping elm where boughs are dripping gold—A drift of autumn crocuses their fairy cups unfold—Strange they seem; a ghostly throng; pale spirits of the Spring. Do they hope on Winter's edge to hear the chiff-chaff sing?

Are they real, or mere illusions of the evening mist—Dream-shapes wrought in lavender and white-veined amethyst? . . . Wraith-like in the grey autumnal dusk they seem to be—Other-worldly in their beauty. Flowers of fantasy.

The Homeward Journey

One road leads over the mountains through storm clouds wild and cold—another runs out to the sunset in a glory of crimson and gold . . . Some go by way of green pastures where the healing waters spring—refreshing the soul that has travelled deep valleys of suffering.

Good is the road that leads forward—to comfort, contentment and rest—and good is the road of adventure, pursuing an unending quest . . . But there is a point of convergence—where my road meets your road, my friend—for we're all on the same homeward journey, and all roads are one in the end.

The Rose and the Frost

The frost that killed the other flowers has beautified the crimson rose. She wears a string of frosted pearls—and in the wintry sunlight glows—red and lovely, standing bravely in a world that's cold and grey. The rose I thought had breathed its last has lived to bloom another day.

The frost of grief can strike the spirit, blighting, freezing, withering—so that in the heart bereft no hope unfolds and no birds sing. But like the rose that has survived the touch of winter's bitter breath—Love remains forever fragrant; Love outlives the change called Death.

OCTOBER 22ND

Rooted

Deep are the roots of a tree on whose tall trunk wide boughs are bourne. Strong is its grip upon the earth, for from the earth its life is drawn. We, too, need roots to hold us steady when the big winds blow—for unless we're rooted we can never really grow.

We need a place where we belong to spread our roots and find—the strength and nourishment required for body, soul and mind. Rootless we crash when troubles come like bolts out of the sky. But rooted we stand with faith unshaken—while the storm roars by.

To Greet Another Spring

The autumn trees are weeping for they know the bitter truth—that they must say goodbye to summer and the year's green youth . . . Leaves of amber, flame and gold are scattered carelessly—by the winds that bring the season of austerity.

Unlike the trees, I cannot grieve when bright leaves fall and fade—because I know that nature's laws must ever be obeyed—so that in the hardened veins of every living thing—the April sap can rise again to greet another Spring.

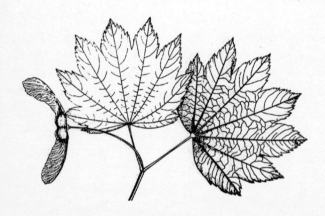

That Is What It Means to Have a Friend

Someone to tell your troubles to when troubles come along. Someone with whom to talk things over when they're going wrong. A prayer to say, a smile to give, a helping hand to lend—that is what it means to have a friend.

Someone to reinforce your courage when it starts to flag. Someone to ease the burden when the spine begins to sag. Someone to keep you going when a mountain you ascend—that is what it means to have a friend.

Someone to share the problem and to help you work it out. Somebody to confide in when assailed by fear and doubt. Someone to give you back your faith when hope comes to an end—that is what it means to have a friend.

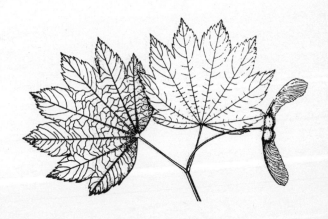

In the Forest

Summer's glory lies in ruins—for the forest is afire—
Richly glows the crimson light on burnished dome and
golden spire. Towers of jade collapse and crumble: walls
of amber crack and crash. Leafy cities of the woodland
fall in clouds of dust and ash.

Rafters of the green cathedrals—roofs of beechen
colonnades—Hang in charred and burning beams
across the blue and smoky glades . . . But Nature's
unseen architects will work in silence day and night—
to build the mansions of the Spring upon this red and
ruined site.

The Garden Hedge

The wind has stripped the garden hedge—and laid its little secrets bare: the closely matted ivy stems; the shoots of bramble twining there; the mossy stones upon the bank—where run the thick roots of the may . . . The birds, no longer screened by leaves—thread in and out from spray to spray.

Robin, sparrow, thrush and blackbird on their daily errands go—gone now is their privacy—their every move I see and know . . . In Summer, safe from prying eyes—behind a wall of living green—But now I look right through the hedge—as though a torn and tattered screen.

Silver and Gold

When the woods grow silent and the summer's tale is told—the silver birches wrap themselves in cloaks of shining gold . . . As if the final hour demanded that they look their best—Going to their winter death in robes of glory dressed.

Slim and graceful, leaning on the wind, they stoop and sway—the loveliest things in all the world upon this lovely day . . . A memory to take into the bitter days and dark—the shimmer of the sun on golden leaves and silver bark.

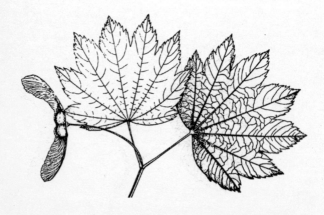

Say It Now

Say the kind word, the word that pleases, charms and cheers. Say it now or maybe you'll regret in after years—you missed the chance of making happy someone dear to you. Take your opportunities, nice things to say and do.

Often unexpectedly and in a way most strange—Life takes on a different pattern. Circumstances change . . . Suddenly without a warning there's a broken thread, and bitter is the thought of deeds undone and words unsaid.

How much kinder we should be to friends and family—if we really grasped the fact of life's uncertainty! . . . Another chance to make amends we think Time will allow—but all too often it's too late—to say the kind word now.

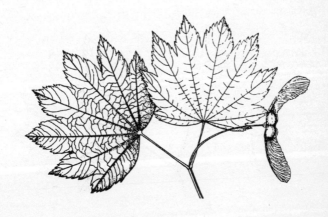

A *Change of Mood*

There's a wintry touch in the air today, a fleck of frost
on the holly spray—and more than a whispered hint of
death in the smell that comes on the wind's rough
breath: the smell of leaves that decaying lie—under the
grey and grieving sky.

But a change of season need only be—a change of
rhythm, a change of key—a different mood and another
phrase—in the symphony of the passing days . . .
Summer and Autumntide, Winter, Spring. Each
has it's own good gift to bring . . . Enjoy then the year
with it's changing themes—thankful because there are
no extremes.

Travel the world and you'll never find—a climate where
Nature is half so kind . . . Gently we pass from
Autumn's glow—to the Winters that bring but a little
snow: a few brief weeks when the birds are dumb—
when the long nights drag and the sharp frosts come—
but even when April seems far away—God often sends
us a beautiful day.

The Great Thought

Lean upon the thought of God, a great thought let it be,
Large enough and deep enough to rest in, utterly.
Finding consolation, hope, refreshment and release
In the quiet comfort of His presence and His peace.

Lean on this, for this alone will take your whole full
    weight.
And will make you strong to face whatever be your fate.
Every other staff and stay will be of no avail.
Lean upon the word of God for this will never fail.

Dead Leaves, Living Roots

The dead leaves flutter from the branches, but the roots
remain: the living roots from which some day the sap
will rise again . . . There will be a resurrection; an
awakening—an Easter morning, green and lovely with
the breath of spring.

The world has had its wintertide of grief and strife and
dearth. War has left a trail of death across the ravaged
earth—But from the grave of past despairs, of bitterness
and pain—God will raise up life anew . . . and men will
smile again.

November

The Gay Pretence

Ankle-deep in golden leaves we walked the beechwood, you and I— conscious of the smoke-blue mist and rooks against the evening sky— Noting every glimpse of beauty: moving cloud and changing light—as the red November sunset burned upon the edge of night.

We played our game of gay pretense although we knew we had to part—Talking of a thousand things . . . but not what lay within the heart. We could not bear the bitter knowledge that our joy had reached its end. We did not probe that agony. It seemed much wiser to pretend.

November 2nd

Fireside Rendezvous

Dream-faces from the shadows smile at me—when from the busy world I draw apart . . . Ghosts cross the threshold of my memory—as I unlatch the doorways of the heart.

Draw the bright curtains on the twilight gloom. Shut out the darkness as the night descends . . . Here in the silence of this firelit room—I have a rendezvous with absent friends.

The Good Investment

Time is Life, so spend it wisely; not on trivialities—but on things that leave behind a trail of lovely memories. Everything depends on Time: work, travel, moon and sun—tides and harvests. Time will not delay for anyone . . . Time flows on from day to day—but one day it must stop. You cannot hoard it in a bank or buy it in a shop.

Time is yours. Don't measure it but treasure it like gold—and a rich endowment will be yours when you are old . . . Invest your time in friendships and a blessing you will earn—Love pays generous dividends and brings a good return.

Fairy Lanterns

In the dense and tangled thickets of the wayside hedges—On the banks along the lanes and by the meadow edges . . . The fairy lanterns now are lit, and hang from every spray; from branch and twig, from stem and sprig the wee lamps swing and sway.

Where Summer's palest roses grew, the ripe red hips are burning—And haws upon the may-bush mark the winter's swift returning . . . On boughs of holly and of yew the crimson berries blaze—giving warning of the coming of the frosty days.

Tea-time

I have drawn the curtains close upon the day's last light—and piled the logs to make a blaze, sufficient for the night. Shadows flicker red and golden on the ingle wall. The tray is on the table and the clock chimes in the hall.

There are crumpets piping hot with butter thickly spread—cherry cakes and ginger snaps and home-made jam and bread. The copper kettle on the hearth is singing merrily—a welcome to the dear old friend who's coming here to tea.

November 6th

The Falling Leaf

The world's unnumbered sorrows and the heart's unuttered grief is expressed in this: the silent falling of a leaf . . . Slowly through the air it flutters as the breeze goes by—if our ears were so attuned perhaps we'd hear it sigh—as it said goodbye to all it would not know again: the glitter of the sunlight and the patter of the rain. Never more to quiver when the passing birds alight. Never more to feel the quick commotion of their flight.

But for every one that falls another leaf will form—when the sap has risen and the days grow bright and warm . . . So it is when teardrops fall. The heart with grief is numb—but later on for every tear another joy will come.

Benediction

The woods are like cathedrals in the grey November days—when the fires of Autumn smoulder to a smoky haze. The beeches stand like stone-grey pillars fading out of sight—into aisles of shadow flecked with gleams of golden light.

High above the dappled paths the arching branches rise—and through their windows shafts of glory strike down from the skies—glowing on the rich mosaics that the leaves have made—yellow, russet, red and green in grove and glen and glade.

Do not miss November's beauty. Go and see it now— before the winter closes in and strips the last bare bough. Walk in Nature's great cathedrals. Listen and you'll hear—God pronounce His benediction on the dying year.

Smoke

Clouds of smoke in cottage gardens. In the damp, grey autumn days . . . Pyres of weeds and red fires leaping— all along the country ways.

Ragged heaps of blighted blossom. Smoking piles of faded flowers—bringing back forgotten glories—of the Summer's golden hours.

Time of burning and destruction. Death to every useless thing—so that man can cleanse the earth—and plan for yet another Spring.

November 9th

Thoughts and Words

Every thought you think and every word you say— sets the trend of life lived out from day to day . . . Everything that comes, unhappiness or joy—affects you by its power to strengthen or destroy.

Thoughts in time create their forms externally—and build the dreams you dream into reality . . . If this plain truth were grasped and rightly understood—Life would change, for thoughts and words would tend towards the good—denying evil's dominance—affirming Love's omniscience.

The Turning Point

There is a milestone on life's path
   that brings us to another start,
where brighter vistas open out,
   where clouds grow light and break apart . . .

There is a spot on every road
   where ruts give place to smooth green ways;
the place that marks a new beginning,
   and the hope of fairer days.

Are you weary of the journey—
   does your burden seem too great?
Are you fighting uphill battles,
   struggling with a hostile Fate?
The milestone at the turning point
   may be a few steps round the bend.
Courage! . . . This may be the spot
   where joys return and troubles end.

NOVEMBER 11TH

Let the Silence Speak

Let the Silence speak, a nation's homage to express
Honouring an ever-sacred debt of thankfulness
To those who gave the gift of life that we might live
  to be
Heirs to the inheritance of British liberty.

Time's grey mantle covers all and memories grow old,
So to every generation let the tale be told!
Tell the world lest it forget the men who fought and
  died.
Bid the Silence speak and let the Dead be glorified.

NOVEMBER 12TH

Winter Never Comes

Day by day around the trees a carpet has been spread—
the last leaves of October, bronze and russet, gold and
red . . . but I refuse to heed the warning of November's
gloom—while there are chrysanthemums in full and
lovely bloom.

Through the grey and gauzy curtains of the foggy
haze—they glow like lamps to light the passing of the
golden days . . . So long as in my garden I can see
chrysathemums—dreams of Summer linger on and
Winter never comes.

You Pass but Once

Once, only once, you pass along this way. So do the good you mean to do each day . . . If it's worthwhile—it's risky to delay. Tomorrow? What may happen? Who can say?

Those well known lines in many a home you see. A little jewel of philosophy . . . "You pass but once" . Your opportunity—is now and here, wherever you may be.

We pass but once! How true those words remain! We're all on the move. We call time back in vain . . . Do not let that good intention wane . . . because you will not pass this way again.

November Roses . . .

Though across the garden now the chilly breezes blow—Still the last late roses make a brave and glorious show . . . Were it not that on the grass the frost lies thick and grey—I would be deceived by them; so bright they are and gay.

Defying death, they lift their heads, untroubled, unaware—As if they had not felt the breath of Winter on the air . . . Their lovely petals open to the cold and sunless noon—as sweetly as they did beneath the golden skies of June.

No Time for Tears

The dead leaves blow along the street. The dying creepers fall. Some say it's a time for tears, the saddest time of all, but I can hear no sorrow in the sighing of the breeze—or see no cause for lamentation in the tattered trees.

This is Nature's wise provision. Things must cease to grow—resting for a season under ice and frost and snow—so they will be ready for the moment of rebirth—when God performs His miracle and recreates the earth.

Towards the Sunshine

Do not let your mind go grey—on a dreary foggy day. Rise above—the weather's whim whether it be bright or grim . . . Take the sunshine where you go. Make it shine and let it show. Other people meeting you—will catch the mood and spread it too.

Don't let Life be coloured by—the changing colour of the sky. Within your mind a compass hold that points towards the blue and gold . . . Learn to like both worst and best. It will help you face the test of life and its uncertainty—with a gay philosophy.

NOVEMBER 17TH

Planting

When you're placing tulip bulbs along the border edge—planting wallflowers in the boxes on the window ledge—setting out forget-me-nots in urns and troughs and tubs—digging holes for saplings or preparing ground for shrubs—you cannot help but wonder how the world will look to you—when these things are flowering underneath a sky of blue.

Planting sends your thoughts across the months that lie between—the gloom of grey November and the first bright April green . . . You know not what the Spring will bring, but this you can aver—that every flower you plant will make it that much lovelier. When you see the things you planted with their buds unfurled—you'll know you've done your own small part to glorify the world.

NOVEMBER 18TH

Bless the Day

Bless the day when it comes to your window—stealing in on the edge of the night . . . Whether it's grey and shrouded in shadow—or sapphire and gold in the first morning light.

Bless the day with a heart that is singing—as with hope the fresh prospect is viewed. . . Bless the day for the good it is bringing—Run to greet it with courage renewed.

NOVEMBER 19TH

Watching the Sun Go Down

Sometimes after fog and frost and skies of leaden grey—
there comes a lovely sunset like a blessing on the day.
Through the leafless trees you see the red and rosy
rays—and before you draw the curtains on the dying
blaze—you pause a moment, thinking of the wonder of
it all: the great world turning from the brightness of
that burning ball—away from all the warmth, the
power, the glory and the light wheeling back into the
darkness that we call the night.

NOVEMBER 20TH

Oak

Late into the dying year the oak leaves linger, green and
gold—as if reluctant to depart, unwilling to release their
hold—upon the boughs that nourished them beneath
the warm blue skies of May. Now on sapless twigs they
hang, the last to fade and fall away.

Oak has gone into the making of our English history;
the cottage home, the stately hall, and Nelson's ships
upon the sea . . . So we have a secret kinship with this
native of our land—for we too have our ancient roots
within the soil on which we stand.

Try a Little Humour

Try a little humour when life's going wrong.
Try a little laughter, try a little song . . .
It will work like magic when you're feeling low—
make a little effort, and the mood will go.

Try a little sunshine on a gloomy day.
Practise painting rainbows on a sky of grey . . .
Don't sit at the window grumbling at the showers—
weave a thread of brightness through the dreary hours.

Do not be despondent when the shadows fall.
Brooding on your problems will not help at all . . .
Fight down the depression and your feelings hide.
Try a little humour, see the funny side.

To Remember

Do not let the greyness of November—seep into the
corners of your mind—There is always something to
remember—something that the summer leaves behind.

The garden: lilac, lavender and roses. Holidays: the
country and the sea—recollect anew as autumn closes—
and live again your lovely memory . . . Grim and grey
the outlook in November—but there's always something
to remember.

The Log Fire

Sometimes when the rustling flames are dancing on the
hearth—I catch the music of the trees along a woodland path
. . . I hear the wind move through the branches in a long low
sigh—and see a tracery of green against a summer sky.

The logs now crumbling into ashes once were sentient
things—Tremulous with life and movement and the beat
of wings . . . The wood that gives its golden fires to
light this wintry day—has worn upon its living limbs
the snowy blooms of May.

Lose Yourself in Other People's Troubles

Lose yourself in other people's troubles—by lending
them a sympathetic ear—for troubles lost perhaps will
be forgotten—and in the end will even disappear.

Lose yourself in what is all around you. The whole wide
world outside your door is there—with neighbours,
colleagues, relatives and strangers—who too have
crosses difficult to bear.

So if you're feeling lonely or despondent—just treading up
and down the same old ways—go take a look at other people's problems—and lose yourself in someone else's maze.

The Argosy

On the broad seas of the future—Out upon the boundless blue—With faith and hope I've launched my ships
. . . Will they return with dreams come true? May the
Star of Fortune shine and guide them safely back to
me—richly laden, sailing into harbours of tranquillity.

Somewhere on the far horizon, battling with the winds
of Fate—There's a good ship homeward bound: the
argosy for which I wait . . . Someday may I see that ship
with all her canvas spreading wide—proud and lovely,
coming home . . . borne in upon the evening tide.

NOVEMBER 26TH

Birches in November

Bare as bone against the skies—the branches of the
birches rise—with their lean and leafless forms—
stripped to meet the Winter storms.

Now their beauty I can see, silver streaked with ebony—
The pale bark shimmers pearly white—caught in
lustrous loops of light. Sentient they seem to be—
Awake, aware, alive to me. I did not know. How could
I guess—that Summer hid such loveliness?

When I Remember You

I remember a thousand things when I remember you:
the firelight glowing on polished oak; a table set for two
. . . The gleam of lamps in a rain-washed street; the
shimmer of wet leaves. The smoky grey of November
nights. The blue of April eyes.

A meeting under a station clock. A song, a smile, a
dance. The muted sweetness of violins: the music of
romance . . . A country walk and a cottage tea; a
window with a view. I remember a thousand things
when I remember you.

Let It Pass and Let It Go

Do not hang on to a grievance. Let it pass and let it go.
Do not cling to hurts and grudges. Life is very short,
  you know.

Bear no malice, never harbour thoughts of bitterness
  or spite—
Whether you are in the wrong or whether you are in
  the right.
You can't afford to let the poison seep right down into
  your mind.

Try to think of something else and very quickly you
  will find
The trouble loses its importance and in time will fade
  away.
So if something riles and rankles turn it out without
  delay.

You must take the generous view however much you've
  been upset.
You've got to let the grievance go. You've got to drop it
  and forget.
If you're hard and unforgiving in the things you do
  and say
How much mercy can you hope for on the final
  judgement day?

White Chrysanthemums

Far into November when the fogs are thick and grey—
The lovely white chrysanthemums their perfect blooms
display . . . Pure as snow and pale as clouds—and yet
our glance they hold—more than all the gorgeous tones
of bronze and red and gold.

Startling in their wintry whiteness—Restful to the eyes—
after all the brilliant colours of the autumn dyes . . .
Nature, ever provident, has paused to scatter here—
White flowers for the burial of the departing year.

Gardens Bring Back Memories

Gardens bring back memories, the thought of bygone
  hours
mingles with the present as you walk amongst your
  flowers . . .
They stir the recollection of some unforgotten place,
and call to mind out of the past, a scene, a voice, a face.

Even when the last rose falls upon the frosted clay,
you catch upon the wintry wind a song of yesterday.
In every corner of the garden something you will see
that evokes within your heart some lovely memory.

December

DECEMBER 1ST

Once Again December

Once again December at the door—brings the thought
of Christmas—as before present, cards, arrangements,
food and drink—but give yourself a little time to think.

Once again you start the old routine—but think of what
this Christmastime could mean. If all men paused to hail
our Saviour's birth—there'd be no war—but Love and
Peace on Earth.

DECEMBER 2ND

For the Evenings

Do not waste the winter hours that lie ahead of you.
For the evenings set yourself a worthwhile task to do.
Use your gifts. Don't let them rust . . . Paint, sew,
embroider, knit. Master something. Study, learn. Don't
be content to sit—gazing at a screen with passive mind
and eyesight strained. Is your life so empty that you
must be entertained?

All too soon Time passes and we call it back in vain.
The wasted hours are precious hours that never come
again . . . So set yourself that task and when the
winter's course has run—you'll see what you've
achieved and you'll be proud of what you've done.

The Holly Tree

In robes of crimson and of green—the shining holly stands . . . A crown of frost upon her brow—and robins in her hands.

A symbol of the festival of peace and joy and cheer— she wears her brightest gown to greet the Christ-month of the year.

DECEMBER 4TH

Time to Go

The last rose lingers on into December—clinging to the skirts of old November—Like a ballerina ageing fast— who wants to go on dancing to the last.

Sad, but proud, unwilling to surrender—dreaming of the heyday of her splendour . . . Tears of rain from off her petals flow—as the cold wind whispers, "Time to go".

Dark Cupboards

I have planted my bulbs in their bright coloured bowls,
And I've put them away in the gloom
Of a little dark cupboard; it's hard to believe
That they'll live in the darkness, and bloom
In a glory of purple, of white and of pink,
From those small thread-like roots in the mould.
I shall watch the great miracle under my eyes
As the close-clustered petals unfold.
There are dark little cupboards in everyone's life
Where we hide all our secrets away—
Griefs, grudges and fears and frustrated desires
Thrust aside from the light of the day.
Could we open our cupboards and bring them all out
Of the darkness—perhaps we should find
The green tips of friendship—fresh flowers of new hope
Growing out of the depths of the mind.

Happiness Waiting for You

There is light at the end of the tunnel
There is calm at the end of the storm . . .
There is rest at the end of the journey,
and a hearth that is welcome and warm.

There's a star on the top of the mountain
you can touch when the last crag is scaled.
There's a certain reward for the faithful
at the point where they think they have failed.

There's a spring at the end of the winter
and behind the black cloud it is blue . . .
There's a song at the heart of your sorrow,
and happiness waiting for you.

DECEMBER 7TH

The Garden of Your Dreams

If you love a garden, winter brings a welcome break—
in which to think about the changes that you'd like to
make. Birdbath, urn or sundial to be placed in different
places—Flowers to re-arrange so they will turn their
sun-washed faces—to the door or to the window.
There's so much to do—in the winter evenings when
you start to plan anew.

However grand this year has been, however bright the
show—you're never really satisfied with what you've
done and so—you go on striving for perfection, weaving
rainbow schemes—always seeing in your heart the
garden of your dreams.

DECEMBER 8TH

One by One

You do not have to take in one great stride—the busy
day that lies ahead of you. When troubles loom around
on every side—and nowhere can you see a clear way
through—Just take it step by step and you will find—
fears fade like snowflakes melting in the sun . . . The
worst things happen only in the mind—and problems
are disposed of one by one.

Whatever Love Demands

When you're running round upon a Christmas shopping spree—buying things for others: gifts for friends and family—remember that affection is the best gift to bestow—affection, love and happiness . . . At Christmas warm hearts glow—and kindly feelings are expressed, but only for a day—when its all over, all too often kind thoughts fade away.

Never salve your conscience with a gift bought at a price. It costs much more to give yourself, for this means sacrifice: time, attention, sympathy . . . Love makes demands on you—not just at the festive season, but the whole year through.

DECEMBER 10TH

The Intruder

A robin redbreast perched upon the mossy headstone of a tomb; an impudent intruder in a place of silence and of gloom.

There amongst the crumbling graves he sang his little melody—making music in the shadow of the solemn cypress tree. And a mourner, passing by, looked up and heard and understood, the meaning of the robin's song: that all was well, and life was good.

The Dreamers

Dreamers can't keep up with those who walk the quickest pace—They like to stroll, while others rush to win life's hectic race . . . Folks who push the rest aside, the hustling bustling kind—forge ahead and seem to leave the dreamers far behind.

But the dreamer sees a lot the other fellows miss—He has time to look around—to feel the sun's warm kiss— Time to watch and time to wonder, pausing here and there—Time to pray and time to ponder, time to stand and stare.

Oftentimes the hustlers flag before they reach their goal—having no resources left of body, brain or soul . . . And the dreamer overtakes them, ambling gaily past— Having come the long slow way, he gets there at the last.

Grey Mornings

Winter brings grey mornings. The sun's up there, no doubt—but the thick cloud hides it and so it can't get out. Looking from your window you see a foggy pall— a thick, depressing greyness hanging over all. Between you and the sunshine—between you and the light— there is a heavy curtain. Beyond the sky is bright—but that is not much comfort when rushing for a train— standing in a bus-queue or walking in the rain.

The weather you can't alter. It's out of your control— but do not let the greyness get into your soul . . . However dark the morning it's still a miracle. To wake and come to life again is always wonderful—a sort of resurrection. In a mysterious way—rising from the death of sleep to live another day.

Jasmine

Yellow stars of winter jasmine round the cottage window fall. Blossom bright as summer sunshine flickers on the red brick wall. In the gloom of bitter mornings it is lovely to behold—when the grass with frost is sheeted and the wind is keen and cold. Coming in the sunless season when no glory lights the skies, bursting on the dreary garden in a moment of surprise.

. . . Like a sudden thought of God that flashes on the darkened mind—when the soul feels lost and lonely in a world that seems unkind. Jasmine flashes hope's bright ray—into the December day.

DECEMBER 14TH

December Days

The days grow shorter as the year rolls on towards it end. Too soon it seems the light grows fainter and the nights descend . . . Brief the journey of the Sun. December days are drear. But they bring us to the morning of another year.

And at this point upon the road the heart is strangely stirred—for far away we hear the music of an April bird . . . With brighter hope and lighter step we tread the wintry hills—having caught upon the wind the breath of daffodils.

The Greatest Gift of All

Ever since Creation's dawn when mankind came to
birth, God has given unto us the rich fruits of the
earth. From His hand we have received gifts great and
wonderful: the harvestings of sea and soil and all
things beautiful.

But not content with all that love had given unto us, He
gave Himself. And in a manner strange and marvellous
was born in little Bethlehem as man with men to dwell:
our Saviour and Redeemer. Jesus Christ, Emmanuel.

DECEMBER 16TH

Sunlight through the Trees

How lovely is the sunlight when through wintry woods
it gleams—and down the grey and silent aisles the
golden glory streams . . . Like some quiet consolation
stealing secretly—on a heart that long has fed on bitter
memory.

We wander in the woods of grief—down lonely paths
we grope—when suddenly upon the gloom there breaks
a gleam of hope—On the way that once was dark the
rays of light descend—and through the trees we see that
there is sunshine at the end.

The Little Rose of Christmas

Now come the Christmas roses. Their wax-white blooms unfold—in December gardens when days are dark and cold. Their pale and ghostly beauty the bitter wind defies—to bring a thought of comfort before the old year dies.

In secret places hiding with snowy petals spread—beneath the frosted bushes where autumn leaves lie dead. They wake while all things slumber, the wintry world to brave—and rising from the darkness they steal out of the grave . . . At this most holy season when sweet the robins sing—the little rose of Christmas comes out to greet the King.

DECEMBER 18TH

Believe

Be not afraid, the Master said. Be of good cheer. Believe! Let not your heart be troubled. Trust in God. Have faith. Receive—the truth revealed at Bethlehem for all mankind to see: the everlasting miracle of the Nativity.

Man for all his cleverness has nothing new to say—to strengthen and to comfort you when comes the evil day . . . Christ alone can speak the Word that saves humanity. I am the Way, the Truth, the Life. Fear not. Believe in me.

The Eyes of a Child

Lovely are the eyes of children, angel-pure and starry bright. Happy, guileless, trusting, candid—shining with the inner light of the uncorrupted mind, by worldly wisdom undefiled. Speak no word to cast a shadow on the clear eyes of a child.

With foolish and indecent haste we force the pace of growth and so—too soon they lose that shining look. Too soon they learn, too soon they grow—Too soon comes knowledge of wrongdoing, sex and vice and violence. Let them be children. Cut not short the springtime of their innocence.

The Story Ever-new

Wild and wintry is December, dark and cold and grey—
but it brings unto the world the Christ of Christmas
Day . . . Once again above the discords of this troubled
earth—angel voices tell the tidings of Messiah's birth.
Never was so sweet a story told by tongue or pen—that
God had come in human form to dwell as man with men.

Not in royal splendour born, with pomp and diadem—
but humbly in the stable of an inn at Bethlehem. And he
who would the truth discover and his Saviour find—
must go with childlike faith and with humility of
mind—kneeling with the shepherds at the manger to be
blessed—for this is the Throne from which He reigns,
the end of every quest.

Christmas is the Time . . .

Christmas is the time when kindly gestures can be made. The time to write the letter that has been too long delayed. The time to break the silence that has fallen between friends. Time to straighten out the tangles. Time to make amends.

Christmas is the time to pay a debt of gratitude. The time for the indulging of a charitable mood . . .The time for being human, sentimental, generous. Once a year it comes and once a year God gives to us—a chance to act out in our lives what Jesus came to teach: a golden opportunity to practise what we preach.

DECEMBER 22ND

In Search of Truth

If you want to find the Truth, the Truth that satisfies— the old, the young, the rich, the poor, the simple and the wise—you must lay aside all pride and in humility seek the truth that lies behind the Christmas mystery.

If you want to find the peace the world can never give— the bread of life to feed upon—a hope by which to live. . . Go you unto Bethlehem the blessing to receive— Kneel before the infant Saviour saying: "I believe".

DECEMBER 23RD

Christmas is for Everyone

There are homes this Christmas where the festive days
will bring—only thoughts of happier times. The
Christmas bells will ring—and wake no echo in a heart
that grief has turned to stone—living through old
memories beside the fire . . . alone.

But Christmas is for everyone—for all need to be told—
the message of the angels. To the young and to the
old—to the one who sorrows and the one whose heart
is gay—God sends His tidings of great joy, declared on
Christmas Day.

DECEMBER 24TH

The Stable Door

They came that night to Bethlehem, the simple and
the wise. The shepherd and the scholar saw the glory
in the skies—and sought the holy manger bed, that
place of mystery—where God Himself had broken in
upon humanity.

The greatest men who walk the earth can offer us today—
no diviner revelation. This then is the Way . . . Though to
knowledge high and vast the human mind may soar.
Every man must come at last unto the stable door.

This Is Christmastide

An island of peace in a sea of turmoil.
  This is Christmastide.
A vision of light in a world of shadows.
  This is Christmastide.
The promise of something that lies beyond
  The torment and the tears.
The glory of God like the rising sun
  Across the long dark years.
An echo of music that seems to come
  From angels hovering.
The wonderful confirmation of
  A strange and lovely thing.
A message that sets all earth and heaven
  Ringing far and wide,
The marvellous message that he is with us.
  This is Christmastide.

DECEMBER 26TH

The Supernatural

Behind the world in which we live: the world we touch
and see—There's a world that opens out into Eternity . . .
There are walls that stand between, but sometimes God
breaks through—telling us of things beyond the range of
human view.

Every inspiration, every flash of love divine—springs
out of a mystery that no man can define . . . On the
common paths of life a sudden glory falls—blazing
brightly for a moment through the phantom walls.

DECEMBER 27TH

Towards the Sun

December is the dreary month that brings the longest
night, the deepest depths of darkness and the shortest
span of light. But once the shortest day is over, changes
come about—week by week we see the wintry twilight
lengthen out.

So December's sombre cloak conceals a lovely thing—
the fledgling hope that warms the spirit with a thought
of Spring. It brings the longest night, but ere the new
year has begun—it brings the shortest day that turns the
world towards the sun.

But the Heart Remembers . . .

The fires of youth may die away and sink to crimson embers . . . The high romantic dreams may vanish—But the heart remembers.

The heart remembers everything; the buried past is there. The rapture of love's first delight; the joy and the despair. The faces and the friendships and the names of long ago—Lie beneath a drift of years like leaves beneath the snow.

The sorrows and the happiness—Gay Junes and grey Decembers. The music fades, the roses perish . . . But the heart remembers.

DECEMBER 29TH

Before the Old Year Passes

Before the Old Year passes—before it breathes its last—Be thankful and remember the mercies of the past. The happiness granted, the benefits untold. The undeserved bestowal of blessings manifold.

Remember too your failings. Recall them one by one: the weaknesses unconquered, the good things left undone—resolving to do better, confessing all your sins—before the Old Year passes. Before the New begins.

DECEMBER 30TH

Memory Lights Her Lamp

Memory lights her lamp upon the threshold of the
Year—Bringing happy thoughts and recollections bright
and clear . . . Her golden beam she sheds across
Tomorrow's darkened door. Absent ones come back
again and friends return once more.

Memory casts a golden ray in every lonely place—we
see old scenes out of the past—a loved and smiling
face—The long forgotten friendship and the name
forever dear—Come back to the heart upon the
threshold of the Year.

DECEMBER 31ST

Here Where the Old Year Ends

Here at the place where the old year ends—Here is the
place to make amends. Dropping old grudges—and
casting aside—Grievances, feuds and foolish pride.

Here where the untrodden path begins—asking forgiveness for our sins. Here at the point where the new ways
start, Here let us pause to search the heart. Here let a
quiet prayer be said—as we face the year that lies ahead.